# Managing Knock Your Socks Off Service

Chip R. Bell and Ron Zemke

Second Edition Revisions by
Chip R. Bell and Dave Zielinski

~~ations by John Bush

**AMACOM**

American Management Association
New York • Atlanta • Brussels • Chicago • Mexico City • San Franciscc
Shanghai • Tokyo • Toronto • Washington, D.C.

Special discounts on bulk quantities of AMACOM books are available to corporations, professional associations, and other organizations. For details, contact Special Sales Department, AMACOM, a division of American Management Association, 1601 Broadway, New York, NY 10019. Tel.: 212-903-8316. Fax: 212-903-8083. Web site: www. amacombooks.org

This publication is designed to provide accurate and authoritative information in regard to the subject matter covered. It is sold with the understanding that the publisher is not engaged in rendering legal, accounting, or other professional service. If legal advice or other expert assistance is required, the services of a competent professional person should be sought.

Library of Congress Cataloging-in-Publication Data

Bell, Chip R.
Managing knock your socks off service / Chip R. Bell and Ron Zemke.
—2nd ed. / revisions by Chip Bell and Dave Zielinski.
    p. cm.
    Includes bibliographical references and index.
    ISBN-13: 978-0-8144-7368-9
    ISBN-10: 0-8144-7368-7
    1. Customer services. I. Zemke, Ron. II. Zielinski, David. III. Title.
HF5415.5.B436 2007
658.8'12—dc22                                           2006032974

MANAGING KNOCK YOUR SOCKS OFF SERVICE® is a registered trademark of Performance Research Associates, Inc.

Artwork © John Bush.

Printing number

10 9 8 7 6 5 4 3 2 1

# Contents

# Preface

Has customer service gotten worse, or have we just become a nation of gripers and whiners?

My father was a big fan of the comic strip "Mutt and Jeff." His favorite had Mutt and Jeff enjoying a bit of verbal sparring. "If everyone saw like I did," boasted Jeff, "Everyone would want my wife." "If everyone saw like I did," quipped Mutt, "*No one* would want your wife."

It was my first lesson on the "eye of the beholder" side of understanding relationships and human experiences. So, when someone asked me the question, Has customer service gotten worse, or have we just become a nation of gripers and whiners?, I thought about my dad's favorite joke.

Remember the scene in the movie *Back to the Future"* when a customer pulls into a gas station circa 1950s and two squeaky clean attendants cheerfully wash the windshield and carefully check the engine fluids? Audiences laughed at the obvious spoof.

Was that great customer service? I don't remember thinking it was back in the 50s and 60s. It was just neighborly care by local employees who had the luxury of being able to serve one customer at a time. They worked for an enterprise with healthy profit margins, friendly competitors, and freedom from having to deal with litigious consumers or impatient shareholders. They served customers with limited choices, modest expectations, and fewer time constraints.

Fast forward to today. Customer care has been crowded to the back of the line by a host of familiar pressures. Profit margins have been squeezed by global competitors, convincing more executives to compete on operational efficiency and become low-cost providers. Cost-containment became the watchword, leading to wholesale outsourcing of customer service functions to low-wage call centers, reduction of customers' toll-free phone access, slashing of value-adding amenities and making service training for front-line employees an afterthought rather than a necessity.

The gradual erosion of personal care and attention in the service experience—the triumph of high tech over high touch—had predictable consequences. In a 2005 study by the Customer Care Alliance of Alexandria, Virginia, for example, 70 percent of American consumers reported feeling "customer rage" as a result of the poor service they had experienced, with 46 percent saying they were dissatisfied with how companies handled their complaints. Much of that unhappiness resulted from customers not receiving explanations, reassurances, solutions—or apologies—for problems they encountered. In other cases the frustration was caused by an inability to find a human being to talk to, regardless of how thorough or prolonged the search.

Yet there are signs of hope amidst the rage. More companies across industries have rediscovered a simple but powerful truth about creating distinction in their markets—consistently treat customers like they're unique and special, and it will quickly set the company apart from the mass of other companies competing solely on price and offering unresponsive or indifferent service. These organizations realize that by crafting systems and policies that play fair with customers, allowing people to feel heard and respected when there are problems, and creating the feeling that the customers' best interests are being looked out for, they build the ultimate competitive weapon: the fervently loyal customer who evangelizes to all within earshot (or Internet connection) about their company.

More leaders also are being won over by the continuing stream of evidence that shows the correlation between engaged employees and happy customers—and the indisputable link between happy customers and healthy profits. Studies done by economists and service researchers leave little doubt: companies rated high on the quality of their customer service regularly keep customers longer, have lower sales and marketing costs (as a result of not having to continually replace customers who've defected due to poor service), and often experience higher return on sales.

So what do Netflix, Nordstrom, Walt Disney World, Starbucks, Progressive Insurance, Wachovia Bank, and Cabela's know that Mayday Airlines, Woeful Healthcare, and Sam's Pretty Decent Car Repair seem clueless about?

We have studied the service greats for many years. Prior to his untimely death in 2004, Ron Zemke (the coauthor of the first edition of this book) conducted pioneering research on the service leadership practices of companies known for service excellence. His studies encompassed thousands of managers in hundreds of companies. Enriched and corroborated by research conducted by others, Ron's body of work forms the foundation of the principles and practices found in this book.

If we've learned one thing from the thousands of managers we've worked with while ferreting out the keys to successful service experiences, it is this: Start with good people or else don't even start. It takes bright, savvy, well-trained, and emotionally resilient front liners to make your service vision a dream come true.

Once you've found them, of course, you have to work hard to keep them. Much of that responsibility falls on the managers' shoulders. Study after study shows that employees leave organizations primarily because of poor relationships with managers, not because of pay, benefits, or other factors. How well you train, coach, and support your people—and whether you show appreciation for the hard work they do each day in the trenches serving customers—makes all the difference, not only in retaining your best employees, but in creating memorable experiences for customers.

Yes, the other factors (which we refer to as operational imperatives) are important. But those factors assume that you have hired people capable of and willing to do the job; people who are eager to learn and excited about the idea of helping you create a special organization . . . an organization distinguished by Knock Your Socks Off Service.

So what do you think? Has customer service gotten better or is there still a long way to go for most organizations? How that question is answered will depend largely on what you and your management colleagues do tomorrow, and all of the challenging and exciting days that follow, to create the conditions that enable your front-line people to consistently delight customers.

Chip R. Bell

# Thanks...

This is the place in the book we reserve to say "thank you." The task is always daunting, not unlike that faced each year by Academy Award winners who struggle to remember and acknowledge the multitudes who contributed to their success.

The most important "thanks" goes to the spiritual coauthor of this book, the late Ron Zemke. We had so much fun crafting the first edition. I was perpetually awed and blessed by his wit, wisdom, and wonderful friendship. He brought an endless curiosity to research and a unique passion to writing—toiling long and late over the precise use of language, never settling for the bland or shopworn when a more engaging, candid, and illuminating way to communicate was possible. I deeply miss his presence, but never take for granted his influence. Thank you, Z Man!

We are lifelong learners in this business of service. Customer expectations are forever in transit, making the path to excellence a journey, not a destination. We thank our clients who continue to teach us through their struggles, failures, and triumphs. They challenge us to remember that the client's enthusiasm is too often dampened by the consultant's wisdom. They remind us that humility and courage are the primary traits of pioneers—and of exemplary service managers.

Dave Zielinski was our world-class editor and vernacular engineer. His superb wordsmithing made partially baked ideas sound wonderful. We are grateful for his excellent craftsmanship and "beyond the call of duty" dedication. Jill Applegate was our detail manager extraordinaire through the first and second editions. She always kept us on task, did yeoman duty tracking down hard-to-find facts, and relentlessly served as the reader who kept us relevant and timely. We could not have done this work without her.

A very special thank-you to the late John Bush. It was a pleasure for us to partner with John over the past 17 years. He never ceased to amaze us with his "capture the essence" creative illustrations. His brilliant artwork became an essential part of the "Knock Your Socks Off Service" experience. His friendship, wry sense of humor, and warm personality will be greatly missed.

Finally, we owe a special thanks to two women who played an instrumental role in bringing this new edition to fruition. Susan Zemke's steadfast and enthusiastic support for Ron's service vision, groundbreaking research, and legacy paved the way for creation of this second edition. Nancy Rainey Bell provided emotional sustenance, compassionate critique, and undying love—as well as frequently "taking up the slack" during the time needed to complete the book.

*To all of you: Thank you.*
*Chip R. Bell*

# Imperative 1
# Find and Retain Quality People

Hire good people and work like heck to keep them on the payroll. Knock Your Socks Off Service starts here or it doesn't start at all.

If you are really serious about serving customers better than your competition, you have to start with people who are willing and able to make that happen. Hiring well means being highly selective. When it comes to creating and maintaining a positive relationship with customers, hiring *nobody* is sometimes better than settling for the first warm body that volunteers to show up for eight hours. You can't end up with satisfied, loyal customers if you don't start with quality people—the kind of people who get as big a kick out of delivering great service as customers do receiving it. Period.

But this is a two-act play. Once found and brought on board, quality people must be kept on board. That means orienting them carefully so they come to understand just exactly what you mean by high-quality service. It also means training them fully in the knowledge and skills necessary for success, giving them challenging assignments, and keeping them interested in the work of the organization. And sometimes it means paying them better than the competition is willing to.

It also means growing them, rewarding and recognizing their accomplishments, sometimes individually or sometimes as a group. It means celebrating their efforts when they go "one step beyond" for their customers.

If you seriously intend to distinguish yourself from the competition by smooth, seamless Knock Your Socks Off Service, you won't accomplish that hiring from the labor pool from hell or by maintaining a payroll that turns over faster than dishwashers in a Las Vegas hotel.

# 1

# Recruit Creatively and Hire Carefully

An ounce of selection is worth a pound of training.
—R.J. Heckman
Director of Talent Management,
Personnel Decisions International

On Interstate 4 southwest of Orlando, Florida, a striking cream and tan building fronts the freeway. A big—very big—sign defines it in one eloquently simple word: casting. It's the Walt Disney World personnel office. That one word says a lot about not just Disney but all companies that are focused on becoming known for Knock Your Socks Off Service. They don't "hire" people for "jobs." They "cast" performers in a "role."

In service-focused companies, customer service jobs are thought of less like factory work and much more like theater. At a play, the audience files in, the curtain goes up, the actors make their entrances and speak their lines, and if each and every cast member, not to mention the writer, director, stagehands, costumers, makeup artists, and lighting technicians, have prepared themselves and the theater well, the audience enjoys the show and tells others about it. Then again, the whole production can be a magnificent flop if just one person fails to do a job on which everyone else depends.

In today's service-driven business world, you are more director than boss, more choreographer than administrator.

3

Your front-line people are the actors, and your customers are the audience for whom they must perform. Everyone else is support crew, charged with making sure the theater is right, the sets ready, and the actors primed and prepared. You have to prepare your cast to know their cues, hit their marks, deliver their lines, and improvise when another cast member or someone in the audience disrupts the carefully plotted flow of the performance. And, of course, once the curtain goes up, all you can do is watch and whisper from the wings. You're not allowed on stage. You'd just get in the way!

## Balancing Efficiency and Effectiveness

Given all the currents flowing under and around the hiring process today, the last thing you want to do is rush into a decision that can make or break how the critics, your customers, rate the quality of your service performances. Once the casting decision has been made, your entire production's reviews are going to depend on the person you've chosen for the role. It's as easy to be taken in by a handsome external facade as by a well-proportioned résumé. Neither may be truly indicative of whether someone can play the part the way you need it to be played.

Yes, the show must go on. But if you've been building a good, versatile cast, you should have understudies ready to fill in while you look for new additions to your service repertory crew. Don't rush the process. Invest the time and effort needed to get the right person. When you do, you'll find you're in good company.

In our research of companies with exemplary service practices we found painstaking thoroughness built into every step of their selection process for service employees. Rather than focusing only on metrics like cost-per-hire or time-to-fill open jobs, these organizations were just as concerned with finding the right fit—in terms of applicants' technical skills and hard-wired attributes like personality and values—for customer contact jobs. Customer-centric companies understand that success in service roles is as much about having the right temperament or the desire and emotional fortitude to deal with customers day in and out, as it is about product knowledge or mastering new technologies. While plenty of job prospects are blessed with good social skills, not all have a high level of *tolerance for contact*, the ability to engage in many successive short bursts of interaction with customers without become overstressed, robotic, or unempathetic.

## Casting a Role, Not Filling a Job

Filling out your service cast with people who can star in their roles is the key to success. But casting your customer service play is far more involved and difficult than hiring "somebody—anybody" to sit in a chair and answer a phone or stand at a counter and take orders. Consider the following three key differences between merely filling a slot and getting someone capable of playing a part.

1. *Great service performers must be able to create a relationship with the audience.* From the customer's standpoint, every performance is "live" and hence unique. It earns the best reviews when it appears genuine, perhaps even spontaneous. And it should never be rigidly scripted and certainly not canned.

- *Implication:* Customer service cast members must have good person-to-person skills; their speaking, listening, and interacting styles should seem natural and friendly and appropriate to the situation—neither stiff and formal nor overly familiar.

- As Jim von Maur, president of Iowa-based Von Maur department stores, says of his own company's hiring philosophy, "My Dad had a theory: We can train them to sell. We can't train them to be nice—that was their parents' job."[1]

---

[1] Ron Zemke and Chip Bell, *Service Magic: The Art of Amazing Your Customers* (Dearborn, MI: Dearborn Financial Publishing, 2003), p. 172.

2. *Great service performers must be able to handle pressure.* There are many kinds of pressure—pressure of the clock, pressure from customers, pressure from other players in the service cast, and pressure from the desire to do a good job for customer and the company even though the two may be in conflict.

- *Implication:* Members of the customer service cast must be good at handling their own emotions, be calm under fire, and not susceptible to "catching the stress virus" from upset customers. At the same time, they have to acknowledge and support their customers' upsets and problems and demonstrate a desire to help resolve the situation in the best way possible.

3. *Great service performers must be able to learn new scripts.* They have to be flexible to adjust to changes in the cast and conditions surrounding them, make changes in their own performance as conditions warrant, and still seem natural and knowledgeable.

- *Implication:* Customer service cast members need to be lifelong learners—curious enough to learn from the environment and the classroom, comfortable enough to be constantly looking for new ways to enhance their performance, confident enough to indulge the natural curiosity to ask, "Why is that?" and poke around the organization to learn how things really work. Those who are comfortable with change and handle it well can be the most helpful to customers and need minimal hand holding from their managers.

To get the right kind of people for your company, you have to (1) know what you're looking for and (2) how to look for it.

## Eight Tips for Casting Well

1. *Treat every vacancy like an open role in a play.* Define the service role you are auditioning people for in terms of the part the new cast members must play and how they'll have to

relate to the other members in the cast. Make people skills and technical knowledge of equal importance in your hiring.

2. *Identify the skills needed for the role.* Once the interview begins, it's too late to start thinking about what you want to learn. Based on the job description and your knowledge of the role you are casting, what traits or personal attributes do you want new cast members to possess? Friendliness? Competence? Empathy? Creativity? Confidence? How will you judge the presence or absence of those traits to your satisfaction? Focus the various stages of the selection process on the real-world skills demanded by the part you're trying to fill.

3. *"Screen test" your applicants.* Try role-playing difficult customer situations with applicants or posing "what would you do if" questions based on the kinds of situations likely to occur on the job. You don't want to listen just for "right" or "wrong" answers. You can train them to use the right words later. Listen for orientation and attitude.

Petsmart, the Phoenix, Arizona-based retailer of specialty pet products, decided to move interviews with job candidates from its back office to the sales floor as a way to better "screen test" their interpersonal skills. Managers now walk applicants around the store, periodically striking up conversations with shoppers and then stepping back to see how the applicant interacts with the customer. The company believes these impromptu "auditions" provide a valuable glimpse into how candidates would function on the job.[2]

4. *Use multiple selection methods.* Remember test anxiety in school? Job applicants get it too. Instead of sifting all applicants through one coarse screen, use a succession of fine ones to help you differentiate. Using a variety of methods also helps counter an over reliance on intuition or gut-feel in the hiring process. As Guy Kawasaki, managing director of Garage Technology Ventures and a major contributor to the early success of Apple Computer says, "the problem with intuition is that people only remember when their intuition was right—

---

[2]Jena McGregor, "Putting Customers First," *Fast Company* 87(2004):88.

---

### Selection Questions

There are no magic questions that automatically illustrate an applicant's character and service outlook. However, there are questions that work better than others at eliciting the kind of information you need to make an informed hiring decision. Here are a few to use or adapt:

- What does giving the customer "superior service" mean to you?
- Let me give you a typical customer service situation we get at Acme. (Describe the situation). How would you handle this type of situation? (Look for attitude, not the perfect solution).
- Tell me about a time when you successfully balanced the best interests of the company with the best interests of a customer?
- We all get weary from time to time from the pressure of dealing with people. What do you do to renew yourself so you can stay "up," fresh and enthusiastic on the job?
- I know I sometimes get uptight when I have to deal with an irate customer. You've had experience with difficult customers—can you describe an example that shows how you might typically handle them?
- What do you like most about being in customer service?
- If you were asked to coach someone brand new to serving customers, what advice would you give that person? What "do's and don't's" would you tell them?

---

truth be told, their intuition was probably wrong as often as right."

Consider:

- *Multiple Interviews.* See your applicants more than once, each time with specific objectives in mind for the interview. In the first interview you're likely to encounter a highly prepared or scripted candidate, but by the second or third interview you'll begin see more of the "real" person who will provide more revealing, high-quality information.

- *Peer Interviews.* In firms where teamwork is valued, it's not uncommon for cast members who will be working with whoever is hired to be trained to do short interviews of their own. Their viewpoints are highly functional. When the project has to be finished under the gun, the person *you're* hiring is someone *they'll* need to work with and depend on.

- *Job-Validated Testing.* Tests that reflect the true nature of the job and assess the key skills needed to do it proficiently are valid, provided they're administered equally and fairly to everyone under consideration. Use them.

- *Job Previewing.* Let applicants spend some time seeing what they're getting themselves into. If they're serious, they'll find ways to better present their qualifications to you. If the job turns out to be something other than what they were expecting, they'll often save you the cost of a bad hire by deselecting themselves. For example, one previewing technique for call center job candidates is to play excerpts of real calls they're likely to receive from customers. Hearing the nature of these calls might cause a few candidates to "select out" of the job, even if they have the requisite skills or background to qualify.

5. *Consider nontraditional sources.* The traditional entry-level work force is shrinking. But the proportion of Americans over the age of 50 is mushrooming. Shrewd organizations are taking advantage of this seismic demographic shift by hiring more retired workers for service roles. With their vast institutional knowledge, calm demeanor under fire, and strong work ethic, people of this generation are often a good fit for customer contact jobs. Harley Davidson, for example, hires back its own recently retired employees for part-time roles like calling customers to gauge how well the company has satisfied their needs and to solicit ideas on how to improve service.

Because they know the company and its products so well, the retirees are able to "generate deeper customer insights while also reinforcing the Harley brand," according to management.[3]

6. *Recruit actively.* Good people may not always find you— often you have to find them. Where have your best people been coming from? Are there others back there equally ready and willing to do the job for you? When you encounter service workers who make a strong impression, don't be shy about handing them your business card and suggesting they get in touch the next time they're ready to make a change. Consider rewarding your people—pay 'em a bounty—for bringing in friends, former colleagues, even relatives who are capable of filling roles in your company. It's often a cheaper and more effective way of finding good talent than using Internet job boards, newspaper ads, or other traditional recruiting tools.

7. *Hire people like the job, not like you.* It's very human to overlay your own personal beliefs, values, likes, and dislikes on the selection process, but it's seldom in the best interest of the customer to do so. Beware of the "cloning" effect, or the tendency to hire people who think, act, look, or share the same background as you. Remember the words of economist Leo Rosten: "First-rate men hire first-rate men. Second-rate men hire third-rate men." (We're sure he'd have said "people" if he said this today.)

8. *Review history with your head; review attitude with your heart.* Customer service is a performing art. You size people up in a job interview or at a social gathering by what your instinct—your proverbial gut—tells you about that person. If your vibes are sending you "disconnect" signals, don't silence them just because you're impressed with an applicant's resume, references, or silver-tongued responses to your questions. If you are getting an uneasy feeling about a prospect, the customer may just share the same reaction. Ask a colleague with a reputation for being a skilled interviewer, or a peer you

---

[3]Richard L. Nolan and Suresh Kotha, "Harley-Davidson: Preparing for the Next Century," *Harvard Business Online,* March 14, 2006.

respect, to sit in on the applicant's next interview to double-check your hunch, and to ensure you're not simply reacting to a personal bias or prejudice.

Success on the "Customer Service Stage" takes a great cast, a super script, great support, and great direction. Never compromise on casting, and never sacrifice rigor in the selection process to a desire to trim hiring costs or fill open jobs faster. Putting the right people in the right roles is critical to everything else in the production.

> You start with good people, you train and motivate them, you give them an opportunity to advance, then the organization succeeds.
>
> —J. W. "Bill" Marriott, Jr.
> Chairman and CEO, Marriott Corporation

# 2

# Paying Attention to Employee Retention

I can think of no company that has found a way to look after external customers while abusing internal customers. The process of meeting customer needs begins internally.

—Tom Peters
Management Guru

It used to be so much easier. You needed a body—anybody would do. So you called human resources. Someone ran an ad in the Sunday newspaper or on Monster.com. People sent résumés and filled out application forms. Someone screened the candidates and selected those who seemed most likely to fit into the corporate culture. You interviewed two, maybe three, people—mostly to double-check what was on the applications and make sure none of them had two heads or tended to scratch in embarrassing places. Then you hired one. A week or two later she showed up, signed a batch of forms, picked up her employee manual, and went to sit next to Sally or Juan or Mary to learn the ropes for a couple of days. And that was that. End of story. If she didn't work out, you simply bade her farewell (or transferred her someplace where her influence would be less noxious) and tried again.

No more. People can no longer be treated as interchangeable parts, necessary but essentially similar cogs for the assembly line. Now people are *both* the assembly line and the product. How well they perform is a key component in your ability to satisfy customers enough for them to want to do business with you again. As we've all been learning (often to our dismay) in recent years, the odds against finding the right amount of the right kinds of people are much higher today than ever before.

Declining birth rates, rapidly retiring baby boomers, and other factors will continue to create labor shortages in many industries over the next 10 years, according to the U.S. Bureau of Labor Statistics. Industries like financial services, health care, manufacturing, and others are already feeling the labor crunch on the front lines.

In other cases the problem isn't a dearth of workers—it's finding enough people qualified to perform increasingly complex service jobs. Consider the job description of today's typical call center service representative. These plate spinners must be masters of multiple technologies and communication methods—telephone, e-mail, instant chat—and be able to manage the emotional labor of dealing round-the-clock with customers, perform sales and service duties, and meet often exacting productivity and efficiency standards. If they are working in overseas call centers, they also need a firm grasp of the business norms, cultural idiosyncrasies, language, and even regional accents of the international customers they're typically serving.

When you consider that the average U.S. high school graduate still can't do a three-step math problem, and that 60 percent of employers rate high school graduates' basic English skills as fair or poor, the challenge is obvious for hiring managers charged with filling service jobs that require an increasingly high level of both technical and people skills.

The labor market for service workers will not only get tighter but progressively older, more diverse, and likely less interested in traditional low-status, low-pay, entry-level jobs.

Your challenge? Find people who can do the job today . . . *and* can keep learning so they can do the job tomorrow . . . *and* can handle customers like a million-dollar salesperson . . . *and* can solve customer problems . . . *and* will act on their own in unique and unusual situations . . . *and* remain poised under pressure, day in and out . . . *and* can be relied on to act in the best interest of the customer without compromising the company.

Of course, once you find these paragons of service virtue, they must be willing to take the job . . . *and* be able to work the hours it demands, including evenings, weekends, and the other odd times your customers think they want to be served . . . *and* be prepared to accept a compensation package you can afford . . . *and* be imbued with a commitment to stay with the task at hand that will allow them to gain the experience to do it better . . . *and* be balanced enough to do the work without burning out on the steady diet of stress and tension that so often goes with front-line service.

## Keeping People Builds Profits

Distinctive service is only possible by hiring people who are a cut above average. Once you find 'em, you have to work like heck to keep 'em—especially those who prove to be your best performers.

Focusing on employee retention makes good business sense, of course, because of the high costs of front-line turnover. A 2005 study by TalentKeepers, a Florida-based consulting firm specializing in employee retention, found more than 40 percent of responding companies reported direct costs of $5,000 to $20,000 to replace a single employee, and 33 percent said that indirect costs of turnover were more than $10,000 per employee. That's not to mention the intangible costs of the stress, headaches, and lost productivity experienced by managers continually faced with replenishing the front lines.

What's more frequently overlooked, however, is the toll that the loss of good performers takes on the customer's perception of quality of service. Seasoned service workers, those who provide a consistently high level of service, are the "go-to" problem solvers in their units and are counted on to mentor new employees. They are worth their weight in gold not just to customers but to their managers, since they often serve as "coaches on the field." Losing these employees can lead directly to customer defections since it takes newly hired workers considerable time to acquire the knowledge or service acumen their predecessors possessed. A study conducted by Marriott Hotels, and featured in an article in the *Harvard Business Review,* found that a 10 percent decrease in employee turnover correlated with a one to three percent decrease in lost customers—and a $50 to $100 million increase in revenues.

## Retaining Top Performers

In moments of candor, service managers will admit that not all of their front-line staff are "created equal"—nor does it constitute a devastating loss if some workers leave the company prematurely. In any given service unit perhaps 10 to 20 percent rate as "star" performers, 50 to 60 percent might be deemed "important but not pivotal," and another 10 to 20 percent are considered poor performers. That's why the most effective employee retention efforts, those that have the biggest payoff in terms of customer retention and enhanced productivity, focus on keeping the strongest performers on board.

Managers at Applebee's restaurants understand that not all turnover at the front line has equal value. They are rewarded not for keeping overall turnover low, but for keeping it low among the restaurant chain's *highest performing employees,* according to *Workforce Management* magazine. Merit pay is linked in part to how well managers retain the top 20 percent of performers (determined through biannual performance reviews conducted by teams of managers) and how effective they are at keeping new hires on board. Managers are expected to retain 80 percent of their top 20 percent group, 70 percent of the "middle 60 percent," and none of the bottom 20 percent, according to the magazine. Those who do the best at retaining these coveted workers are feted with awards and recognition at Applebee's annual conference.

Has the incentive program worked? In 2003 it helped Applebee's retain 80 percent of hourly employees and 90 percent of lower-level managers in the top performing categories.

## The Best Retention Tool of All: Good Management

Pacesetting service companies use a host of techniques to keep their top service talent content, motivated, and on board as long as possible. They use training not only to educate but to motivate. They use dual-career tracks to keep top performers doing what they do best while providing them with satisfying growth, variety in their work, learning opportunities, and financial rewards. They educate managers to the new realities of the work force to make sure they understand that service people bruise easily and that good ones are too precious to waste through managerial abuse.

As the labor market for skilled customer contact workers continues to tighten, more and more managers are making the connection between satisfied customers who keep coming back and the loyal, motivated people who provide the service that brings those customers back. Increasingly, keeping good people is treated as a critical concern by the service focused, recession or boom:

• At Walt Disney World, job rotation, cross-training, and the clearly observable fact that the road to management starts at the front line combine to give the entertainment king an enviable front-line turnover rate. In an industry known for triple-digit employee attrition, Disney's employee retention rate is in the 70 to 80 percent range, and it features a customer return rate of more than 90 percent.[1] At pharmaceutical company Bristol-Myers Squibb, a retention "scoreboard" helps managers focus on reducing the resignations of key talent. To improve its ability to keep top performers on board, the organi-

---

[1]Brent VanParys, "The Magic of Marketing," *CAMagazine.com,* December 2005.

zation is raising managers' awareness of the need to more fully engage the workforce, build trust, improve communication of goals, and recognize people for their contributions.

• In Embassy Suites properties, front-line people are rewarded with raises for learning new jobs by cross training that's available to them even when no immediate openings are projected. This learning-and-earning incentive keeps turnover of front liners among the lowest in the industry (and provides an emergency staffing pool ready to respond at a moment's notice).

> Nine out of ten factors influencing employees' decisions to stay are influenced by their managers, not pay or other issues.
>
> —Peter Fasolo, Vice President
> for Human Resources, Cordis Corp.

# 3

# Keeping Your Best and Brightest

We know that if we treat our employees correctly,
they'll treat the customer right.

—J. W. "Bill" Marriott, Jr.
Chairman and CEO
Marriott Corporation

The connection between retaining your best service performers and creating happy customers is powerful and cuts across
virtually every dividing line: industry, size of company, scale
of market, you name it. It's not difficult to see why.

• Customers want and value reliability, efficiency, and
consistency in their service experiences with you with the appropriate dose of friendliness and caring. From the *customer*
standpoint, dealing with experienced people is basic to building a relationship—a true partnership. The truth is it's difficult to get quality service from people who haven't been with
an organization very long.

• Good teamwork comes from working together long
enough to learn the strengths and weaknesses, special quirks,
and predictable habits of other members of the team. As service
becomes more complex and service relationships grow to touch
multiple levels and layers in the organization, internal coordination becomes an important factor in external satisfaction.

- Finally, experience is still the best teacher—no Web-based training module or classroom session can hope to replicate the database that resides squarely between your employees' ears, the tacit knowledge that can only be gained by working on the front lines week after week, year after year, dealing with every customer question, demand, or complaint under the sun. Your true "personnel cost" is much more than a salary total. It's every dime, every minute, every ounce of energy anyone in your organization has spent recruiting, interviewing, hiring, training, supervising, coaching, and profiting from your people.

It's not just common sense that tells us there's a strong correlation between employee retention and organizational performance—a number of studies bear it out. In his book *The Loyalty Effect: The Hidden Force Behind Growth, Profits and Lasting Value*, author Fred Reichheld, director emeritus at the Boston-based consulting firm Bain and Company, reports that when one organization examined the connection in its stores between employee loyalty and productivity, it found that the top third in employee retention were also in the top third in productivity—their sales were also 22 percent higher than stores ranked in the bottom third of retention. A study of fast-food chains in Reichheld's book found that outlets with low staff turnover had profit margins that were more than 50 percent higher than stores with high turnover.

We're not suggesting your goal should be to create lifetime service employees. People change jobs today the way they change credit card providers, and the reality is that many customer service positions are still looked upon as stepping stones to bigger things. The more prudent stance, retention experts say, is to identify the "tipping point" for your front-line staff—the length of employment where turnover most often occurs—and to pull out the stops to convince your top performers, those who are most competent, caring, and resilient, to stay with you beyond that juncture.

Employees who are only with you in body and not in spirit, however, can do more harm to your company's reputation for service quality by staying than by leaving. If repeated attempts to help elevate their performance or change their attitudes fall short, they should be encouraged to look for new opportunities elsewhere in the company or be let go.

## Customers Are Watching

Just as your style of service determines if you'll retain a customer, your style of managing is basic to the retention and service achievements of your people. Yet we all know that there are managers who still use their authority as a club to beat the drive, the sense of fun, and the risk-taking out of people.

Not only does this have a profound effect on the people we manage, it also has an effect—typically more direct than we give it credit for—on customers. If you've ever stood at a checkout counter, held captive by a supervisor who deems it more important to chastise a clerk about yesterday's pricing error than to ensure you get prompt service, you've seen the downside of service management in action.

In several landmark studies, service researchers Benjamin Schneider and David Bowen have shown that *customer service satisfaction* is directly related to *employee job satisfaction*. Their work, done jointly and independently over a 10-year period, points to a number of specific ways that job satisfaction is tied to customer satisfaction:

1. *Customers "see into" the organization through a unique window: the actions and words of front-line employees.* They assume the attitude and treatment they experience at the front line of an organization is an accurate representation of the way the organization wants customers to be treated.

2. *The treatment that customers experience directly reflects the treatment employees receive from their managers.* The "kick-the-cat" phenomenon is real. If you're at the front line and your boss shows you little respect, fails to listen or gives you a hard time, you pass that treatment on—sometimes to other employees, sometimes to family, and sometimes to customers.

3. *On the whole, employees want to give good service and receive customer accolades for it.* When conditions prevent or

prohibit them from doing what they believe to be in the best interests of the customer—when company policies are overly restrictive or managers refuse to even consider viewing situations through the customer's eyes—they become defensive and prickly.

On the positive side, Schnieder and Bowen have found in their work that employees and customers both rate service quality highest in branches of an organization where (1) there is an enthusiastic service emphasis, (2) branch managers emphasize the importance of service to branch success, (3) there is an active effort to retain all accounts, not just "high net" customers, (4) the number of well-trained front-line people at the branch is sufficient to provide customers good service, (5) technology is well maintained and supplies are plentiful, and (6) employees believe they have a reasonable opportunity for career advancement in the organization.

Only when the economics of the workplace are such that there are few jobs and a lot of people wanting them, will people put up with anything just for a paycheck. But as soon as conditions improve, the ones with gumption, initiative, and talent—the ones you really want to keep because they're the hardest to find and replace—will be gone. The question you have to answer is if you want to depend on crisis conditions for employee retention or look for a better way.

## Top Ways to Retain

As a manager, you have a variety of tools to use to keep your employees coming back:

• *Good management trumps all.* Survey after survey shows that people don't leave organizations, they leave bosses. Research from TalentKeepers, a Florida consulting firm, found that while employees are attracted to organizations for factors such as pay, benefits, reputation or the nature of the job itself, within short order it's the quality of their relationship with managers that matters most. If front liners are respected, listened to, provided good working environments and recognized for their hard work, and if managers routinely keep their promises and take responsibility for company policies, it often holds more value in employees' eyes than promotional opportunities, compensation, or health benefits (unless they are paid well below market averages). Conversely, when people are treated like interchangeable parts or simply "butts in seats," managers will usually be rewarded with a marginally productive, listless, and resentful workforce that will leap at the first new job opportunity that promises they'll be treated more like sentient life forms.

• *Compensation and Benefits.* While money may not be everything, it's a very close second to whatever's first. Service-distinctive organizations not uncommonly pay above the average for their industry, using the tactic (1) to attract good people and (2) to keep top talent from seeking greener pastures. FedEx package sorters start out at about double the minimum wage, and even part-timers are eligible for bonuses and profit sharing. Costco warehouse stores pay their full-time hourly workers significantly more than rivals like Sam's Club, the Wal-Mart subsidiary, believing it will result in reduced turnover and greater productivity. A recent study by *Business Week* bears out Costco's thinking. The magazine crunched the numbers of both Costco and Sam's Club, and found that "by compensating employees generously to motivate and retain good workers, one-fifth of whom are unionized, Costco gets lower turnover and higher productivity." Costco's labor costs also proved lower than Wal-Mart's as a percentage of sales, and its hourly workers in the United States sell more per square foot. On the turnover front, the *Business Week* study found only 6 percent of Costco employees left after their first year on the job, compared with 21 percent at Sam's Club.[1]

Other service-focused companies use attractive benefit packages, including company-paid healthcare, to lure and retain

[1]Stanley Holmes and Wendy Zellner, "The Costco Way," *Business Week,* April 12, 2004.

the part-time workers that are essential to executing their service strategies. Seattle-based Starbucks was among the first organization to offer health benefits to part-timers, and companies like United Parcel Service (UPS) and Wegmans Food Market chain, with stores in northeastern and mid-Atlantic states, have since followed suit. Starbucks regularly cites its benefits, which includes a retirement plan, paid vacations, a free pound of coffee weekly, and health benefits as key to a turnover rate that is well below the norm for part-time employees. Health insurance proves to be a particularly strong draw for single parents and older workers not yet eligible for Medicare—a part of the labor pool that might otherwise balk at jobs that pay ten to twelve dollars per hour.

• *Special Treatment.* In lieu of money, respect for individual concerns can compensate in a variety of ways. Instead of forcing everyone to fit into the same employee box, recognize that people each need and value different things. For parents with young children, for example, it may be flexibility around day care, and for those whose children are a little older, it may be the opportunity to attend an occasional school program in the middle of the afternoon. For employees with aging or infirm parents, flexing work schedules so they can provide much-needed care or transportation can prove a big benefit. Ditto for opportunities to telecommute or occasionally work out of a home office.

• *Special Contracts and Perks.* Tie specific types of performance achievements to specific payoffs, whether monetary or symbolic. A "piece of the action"—the increased revenue from a formerly static account that's now growing, or the savings from a suggestion—tells your people you value their efforts. Similarly, tickets to athletic or cultural events, enhanced discounts on the company's products and services, and other "spiffs" keep them from feeling taken for granted.

• *Training.* For today's knowledgeable workers one of the most enlivening and enriching experiences is training that helps them do their jobs better. They know performance counts and that in many cases they're being judged on how well their customers say they're serving. Developing new talents or getting a refresher on old ones helps them stay on top of their game. It also communicates the organization's continuing commitment to them.

- *Cross-Training.* The more hats your people can wear, the more valuable they can be to the organization. If their current specialty goes away or is de-emphasized, they know and you know that they're ready and able to fill an emerging need instead of filling out an application for unemployment insurance. What's more, having people pretrained for other jobs helps you meet unexpected demands, from the need to replace someone who departs unexpectedly, to coping with the occasional (and unpredictable) overload situation, to the ability to respond quickly to new demands and opportunities. People also appreciate the change of pace provided by doing other jobs or tasks, even for short periods.

- *Lateral Job Movement.* The most exciting and fulfilling job becomes stagnant and predictable over time. At many best-of-breed service companies, lateral "developmental assignments" are used to challenge, reward, and motivate people who can't move up (because so many layers of "up" have been eliminated in recent years). Giving your people the opportunity to move laterally not only gives them a chance to rise to a new challenge but helps them gain a new perspective on what they've been doing.

- *Empowerment.* According to Richard Leider, author of *Repacking Your Bags* and *The Power of Purpose*, one of the biggest problems today isn't burnout—it's "rustout." So many people in our organizations are capable of doing so much more than we've ever asked (or allowed) them to do. So let 'em. The more ownership they assume for the responsibilities built into their job, the more likely they are to stay with it, no matter (and perhaps because of) how challenging they find it.

- *Reward and Recognition.* What gets rewarded gets repeated. If you want people to stay and grow with you, recognize and reward them, not just for their years of service but for their accomplishments along the way. For most people, the research shows that being thanked for a job well done is a more powerful motivator than money. It says you're paying attention to their individual (or team) performance, that you recognize how hard they're working, how much they're contributing, how emotionally taxing it can be to deal with customers each and every day, and how valuable they are.

> We have a belief that our guests will only receive the kind of treatment we want them to receive if the cast members receive that same kind of treatment from their managers.
>
> —*Walt Disney World Handbook*

# Imperative 2
# Know Your Customers Intimately

You subscribe to all the trade journals. You do an annual survey of your customers. The company even has done some market research, a couple of surveys, some focus groups. You sit next to the people on the phones from time to time. You yourself jump in and work with tough customer problems when asked. You regularly talk with the salespeople to learn what they are hearing from their customers, prospects, and suspects.

You *are* close to the customer—right? Perhaps. And then again, perhaps not.

Knowing your customer intimately means more than having a passing acquaintance with the market research of your industry or company. It means spending time listening to, understanding, and responding, often in unique and creative ways, to your customers' evolving needs and shifting expectations. Knowing your customer intimately means that people at *all* levels of the organization find time to meet with, listen to, and learn from customers in highly focused ways. Knowing your customer intimately means knowing each other's business so well that you can anticipate each other's problems and opportunities—and can work on solutions and strategies together.

# 4

# "Emotionalizing" the Yardstick: Why Customer Satisfaction Isn't Enough

Customers perceive service in their own unique, idiosyncratic, emotional, irrational and totally human terms. Perception is all there is.

—Tom Peters
Management Consultant

For as long as we can remember the promised land of service-focused organizations—the accomplishment that, once achieved, suggested they'd arrived among the ranks of customer service exemplars—has been represented by two sought-after words: *customer satisfaction*.

When customers report being "very satisfied" or "satisfied" on our surveys, we take it as a sign of their continued loyalty, believing they'll continue to spend their dollars with us and recommend us to others. Yet the truth is that while satisfying customers beats the alternative, it is rarely enough to produce the kind of devoted clientele that will stay committed to your company in the face of new price-slashing competitors, the periodic hiccup in product or service quality, or other threats to their continued patronage. Consider what the word *satisfaction* really connotes. Webster's defines it as "good enough to fulfill a need or requirement," and common synonyms are "sufficient" and "adequate." Hardly the stuff of inspiration.

As service quality researchers have discovered in recent years, measures of satisfaction are often poor predictors of the most important yardstick of any service effort: Will customers not only come back for more, but go out of their way to recommend you to others?

## Love That Customer

Consider the perspective of Robert A. "Bob" Peterson, who holds the John T. Stuart III Centennial Chair in Business Administration at the University of Texas, Austin. His opinion, based on his own research, is that "love that customer" is pretty powerful stuff.

For years, Peterson was troubled that so many people were talking about the joys of customer satisfaction, but his research wasn't showing a very strong connection between satisfaction and retention—repeat business. He found that in most surveys of customer satisfaction, something around 85 percent of an organization's customers claimed to be "satisfied" with the service they received but still showed a willingness to wander away to other providers if the mood, or the price, or the color of the advertising banner were right.

Peterson believes that we have undervalued the emotional aspects of customer service; that there is a highly personal, subjective agenda that we fail to ask about in customer research and fail to deal with in service delivery. Only by adding words like *love* and *hate* to our surveys, and having the audacity to stand up to the need to incorporate much stronger feelings than *like* and *satisfaction* in our objectives, can we get a handle on this crucial component of customer loyalty. And the only way to get to the heart of the matter is by getting our information straight from customers: from their own selfish (and sometimes flawed) perspectives, based on their own experiences, expressed in their own words.

The payoff is the kind of in-depth understanding that can help nurture a truly productive relationship—or save one from going bad. Peterson believes that customers with strong feelings about the organization are the most predictable customers. "Customers who feel strongly about your organization—positively or negatively—are the customers *most likely* and *least likely* to do business with you again," he says.

Recent research by the Gallup Organization corroborates and builds on many of Peterson's findings. In a *Harvard Business Review* article titled, "Managing Your Human Sigma"[1] John H. Fleming, Curt Coffman, and James K. Harter of Gallup examined the nature of employee interactions with customers and found that emotions had a significantly larger effect on parties' judgments and behavior than rational thinking did.

The Gallup team found that customers who rate themselves as "extremely satisfied" on surveys fall into two distinct categories: those who have a strong emotional connection to the company and those who do not. In a multiyear study of hundreds of companies and millions of customers and employees, Gallup found that:

- "Emotionally satisfied" customers contribute far more to the bottom line than "rationally satisfied" customers do, even though the latter rate themselves as equally "satisfied" on customer surveys.

- Surprisingly, the behavior of rationally *satisfied* customers looked no different from that of *dissatisfied* customers. In a large U.S. bank in the study, the attrition rate of dissatisfied customers was on par with that of rationally satisfied customers, or those who described themselves as extremely satisfied but scored low on an "emotional attachment" metric. The

---

[1] John H. Fleming, Curt Coffman and James K. Harter, "Managing Your Human Sigma," *Harvard Business Review,* July-August, 2005.

attrition rate of bank customers who were emotionally satisfied, however, was on average 37 percent lower.

• For all types of companies in the research, Gallup
found that emotionally engaged customers delivered a 23 percent premium over the average customer in terms of profitability, revenue, and relationship growth.

## Measuring via Customer-Derived Language

Does this mean you should start sprinkling words like "love,"
"enchanted," "awful," or "hideous" on your customer surveys? What about the implications for organizations with
lesser aspirations, where in their minds moving the needle
from *"somewhat satisfied"* to *"satisfied"* might represent a
quantum leap in service quality? Is it even realistic to think
you can evoke customer passion or love when you're selling
more pedestrian products or services, those that meet basic
needs but do little to excite or inspire?

How customer expectations change based on the nature of
business transactions can provide some guidance on the language you opt to use on surveys. Consider what customers experience when they purchase an everyday household product
versus when they engage in a more emotion-laden service experience. We buy many of the products we do to meet basic
needs. In purchasing a new refrigerator, trash compactor, or
bed, for example, we usually want to fulfill simple requirements—to keep food cold, dispose of trash, or facilitate comfortable sleep. To be sure, there are some purchases—a Harley
Davidson motorcycle, Apple *Ipod* or women's Manolo Blanik
shoes come to mind—that create an emotional bond and may
border for some on a religious experience, although such
products are in the minority.

Now think about a service experience like a night at a five-
star restaurant, a guided whitewater rafting trip, or even your
own honeymoon. Recalling your fondest memories of the experience, it's unlikely that the highest measure on most surveys—"completely satisfied"—could truly capture your feelings about the experience.

What separates most service experiences from product purchasing scenarios—and what should act as a guide for how you craft surveys to gauge customers' repurchase intentions—is that the service is performed or occurs in a way that physically involves the customer. Imagine that a customer who needed a trash compactor showed up at the factory to help the manufacturer produce the compactor that the customer ultimately planned to purchase. Sound ludicrous? This is how service happens every time.

For example, if a customer gives a "completely satisfied" rating to his five-star restaurant experience, managers of that restaurant are likely to view that as a service and word-of-mouth-marketing coup. But if applied to the emotional yardstick we've described throughout this chapter, it might truly only be a "C" grade in that customer's eyes, meaning the restaurant fulfilled base requirements but barely passed muster. This explains why, as the Peterson and Gallup research confirms, the majority of customers who leave one organization to go to a competitor say, when asked, that they were "satisfied or completely satisfied" with the organization they just left behind.

Shifting from a satisfaction paradigm to one that more closely matches how humans judge a service experience is only part of the solution. The need for reliability in market research techniques can't be sacrificed even if the thing you are evaluating is more subjective. Trusting one customer's definition of "awesome" to be comparable to another's, for example, is questionable science.

The key to improving the measurement process—to get a more accurate reading of how service experiences impact loyalty—is to seek out and use the language of the customer, not of the researcher. If "awesome" is the word that customers use to describe the service experience, then "awesome" it should be. Such customer-derived language will be inexact and slippery. But one way around that challenge might be to begin asking respondents to recall their very best service experience and use the word or phrase that best characterizes it. That word could then be used for the upper end of the scale for all other questions asked in telephone or face-to-face interviews.

Repeating the process for the lower end provides the same semantic differences in the customer's language. This methodology enables Customer A's "excellent" (his highest rating) to be reliably compared to Customer B's "outstanding" (her highest rating).[2]

## Romancing the Customer

Even in traditional manufacturing (and manufacturing-style services), where "careful is correct and rational is right" has long been the managerial axiom, service quality is being recognized as the marketing edge that can differentiate one commodity offering from another. The service tide in which we've all been swept up makes it imperative that we pay increasing attention to whatever it takes, one-on-one and one-by-one, to earn the love and loyalty of our customers.

We don't have the luxury of putting off this transformation. Inspired by their years of experience, well-publicized product quality improvement efforts and heightened service delivery rhetoric alike, customers are getting increasingly emotional, even passionate, about their service experiences. Listen to the raves of the Nordstrom, Cabela's, Netflix, Starbucks, Apple, Amazon.com, and Whole Foods faithful and you'll hear more "love stories" than you'll find on the drugstore paperback rack. Listen, as well, to the tales of anger and woe told by disgruntled customers, and you'll find that novelist Stephen King doesn't have a corner on horror stories.

In this time of passion, how do you use the concept of "customer intimacy" to create long-term loyalty? Start by seeing customer transactions not as a random collection of single experiences, but as a relationship. Relationships in business, just as those in our personal lives, are built on knowledge, caring, and experience. Today segmentation, personalization, and niche marketing are the name of the game in virtually every industry sector. Customers are no longer shapeless, fea-

---

[2]Chip Bell and John Patterson, "I Can't Get No Satisfaction," *Customer Relationship Management*, July 2006.

tureless mass markets. They're specific, small groups with their own unique view of what constitutes quality service. What they want and how they want it—and how they do or don't get it—add up to an index of "customer love" that ultimately determines if they'll ever come back and do business with you again.

It's an adjunct of the Rule of Psychological Reciprocity: If you don't show interest in your customers, they won't show interest in you. If you don't trust them, they won't trust you. And if you don't care passionately, sincerely, constantly about not just meeting but exceeding their needs, they won't see you as being any better or any worse than any other organization they have done business with. They most certainly won't fall in love with your organization.

In short, "ya gotta love that customer" if you expect them to love you back.

> The more brilliant we become on how we perform our jobs, the more inward-focused we can become and the more we need our customers' creativity. It's difficult for service people on the inside to view our service delivery system with the same naive, unbiased, and fresh perspective our customers possess.
>
> —John Berry
> COO, Virginia Blue Cross-Blue Shield,
> Roanoke, Virginia

# 5

# Listening Is a Contact Sport

Two ears, one mouth—you do the math.

—Unknown Author

Listening well is a rarity in our society. That helps explain the popularity of psychologists, the scale of the divorce rate, and why there are so many self-help books with communications as their central theme. As a manager you have to serve as listening post and traffic analyst. Neither is as simple as it sounds.

Part of the challenge of listening is filtering out the noise of bias and defensiveness. When your front-line workers hear customers suggesting ways your business could do more for them, the instinctive response is to determine how much additional work that might mean. When service employees hear negative comments from customers about their or the organization's service performance, they have a natural tendency to defend and protect.

Their inherent sense of "possessiveness" about the delivery system and their tendency to take complaints as a personal attack make it harder for people at the front line to listen in a nonjudgmental way. Although your people are up close and personal with customers on a day-to-day basis, as a manager you are in a better position to listen effectively. Being one step removed from the action, you should have less defensiveness and a broader perspective than the immediate moment.

In addition, front-line workers typically listen to customers for cues on what to do in what order, instructions for tasks to be completed, or requests for problems to be solved. The "immediate action required" nature of this exchange makes it difficult to spot themes and trends at the front line. As a manager, you're more likely to have a forest-wide perspective than a tree-by-tree view.

## Listen, Understand, Respond

Listening does not mean simply looking at someone while they talk, or adding the obligatory "uh-huhs" in the right spots during phone conversations, and then doing something in response. There's an important middle piece to the puzzle: Listening means actively seeking to understand another person. That's why we say it's a contact sport. Listening without contact, listening without a *dramatic connection*, is like looking without seeing. Given the uniqueness of being really heard, customers long remember those front-line workers who listen well.

Active listening is responding in a way that says, "I understand what you are saying; dramatic listening is responding in a way that communicates, "I understand what you are saying *and* I value what you are trying to communicate." Whether focused on questions, complaints, or collecting new ideas, dramatic listening leaves customers with the rare feeling of being heard and confident your organization will honor the information received, taking action where warranted.

Many organizations like to boast of their commitment to great customer listening, pointing to stacks of survey research to prove how serious they are about capturing the voice of the customer. Yet the reality is today's customers, and the employees who serve them, too often feel over-surveyed and under-valued. They sense that companies are going through the motions in seeking their input, simply checking off the box marked "touched base with customers" and then returning to business as usual, giving little consideration to their input. Many of these listening strategies seek facts but not feelings, conversation instead of candor. Only by having the courage to ask for unvarnished opinions from customers—and then listening without donning defensive armor—can you hope to get the kind of honest feedback that leads to meaningful service improvements.

It's also important to listen to the things your front-line people can tell you about constantly changing customer needs and expectations. In settings from Walt Disney World to the call centers of USAA Insurance and televised shopping service QVC Inc., customer contact people debrief each other periodically to spot new problems or requests, emerging opportunities, and the influence of larger market conditions. When managers act on their information, the message comes through loud and clear: Pay attention to your customers. We're interested in what they're telling you. That's how we learn to serve them better.

## Six Ways to Listen for Consumer Needs and Expectations

There are lots of ways to listen to your customers—and to do it well, you need to master and use more than one style. It's like using a belt and suspenders to hold up your pants. The redundant systems reinforce each other, but they do so in different styles with different strengths and weaknesses. Consider the following.

1. *Face-to-Face.* More and more managers are uncomfortable with the idea that the information they are getting is indirect. They want to know things directly and personally, to see and hear for themselves what customers are experiencing on the front lines. Such first-hand knowledge can provide the kind of insights, and make the kind of impact, that reading static customer satisfaction reports never can.

One health care executive we know of makes a point of spending one day a week on the front lines of his hospital, often wearing a volunteer's anonymous coat to reduce the odds that people will slant what they're saying because they know who's listening. Interestingly, he says the customer he's listening to isn't just the patient. He listens to his people, too. His reasoning is simple: His personal customer isn't the patient, it's his people, because those people treat the patients, he doesn't.

Maxine Clark, the CEO of Build-a-Bear Workshop, the unique business that allows children to build their own stuffed animals, visits two to three of the franchises per week, chatting up customers and touching base with employees. Clark says a key to her success as a leader is "never forgetting what it's like to be a customer" of the store.[1]

Front liners and managers can learn a lot about the customer experience simply by being more observant. One hotel chain instituted a "follow me" program that had front desk clerks ask repeat guests if they would, for a discounted rate, allow the bell man to unobtrusively hang around and "watch you unpack and settle in."

The program proved a major source of learning about the small, irritating "workarounds" that hotel customers faced, things like having to place the suitcase of a traveling companion on the floor because the hotel only provided one luggage rack, having to unplug and find a place for hotel-provided hair dryers when guests bring their own, and much more. By "listening with their eyes," hotel employees found ways to enhance the customer experience that guests may never have suggested on comment cards.

2. *Layered Group Listening.* How many times have you had a front-line employee tell you, "I wish you could have heard this complaint. We've been getting it a lot, and I think it's something we really need to fix." Layered group listening is a variation on the focus group technique that enables layers of the organization to listen to customers at the same time. In

---

[1]Lucas Conley, "Customer-Centered Leader: Maxine Clark," *Fast Company,* October 2005.

Figure 5-1, the Xs represent customers, the Os are front-line employees and the □'s are supervisors and managers.

The listening process can be done in three rounds, each lasting forty-five to sixty minutes. In round one, the customers (Xs) are interviewed by a focus group leader. Front liners (Os) can only ask questions for clarification, they cannot explain or defend, and managers (□'s) cannot say anything, they only get to listen. After the first round, customers leave and the Os move to the center table, □'s move to where Os had been and the second round occurs—front liners reacting to what they heard from customers; managers only asking questions for clarification.

In round three, front liners and managers spend a round problem-solving based on what they learned together. Some organizations also find it valuable to bring customers back to participate in this third round.

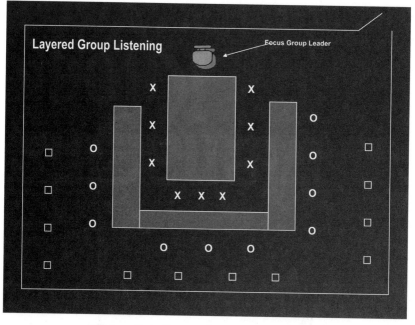

**Figure 5-1.** Layered Group Listening.

The upshot is managers get a first-hand understanding of the frustrations, concerns, and plaudits that front-line employees hear customers voice every day. Sometimes it takes such exposure, hearing straight from the horse's mouth, for managers to truly grasp how service problems are affecting customers' willingness to keep doing business with a company. On the flip side, it's also heartening to hear kudos about the positive things your staff has done to win customers' loyalty or make them sing your firm's praises to others.

3. *Comment and Complaint Analysis.* Some customers will tell you what's on their mind face-to-face. Some won't risk the chance of confrontation or embarrassment, but will fill out simple "Tell Us, Rate Us, Help Us" comment cards. Tracking them can give you a continuing barometric reading on how you're doing. More extensive contacts, like complaint and compliment letters, can be mined for detailed insights into past experiences and future preferences.

4. *Multichannel Response Systems.* Make it easy to listen by making it easy for customers to contact you by using 800 numbers, e-mail, Web-based text chat and more. Most service-focused companies today have Web-enabled call centers that route, queue, and prioritize incoming e-mail from customers, enabling customer service reps to handle e-mail and real-time Web requests as efficiently as calls to 800 numbers.

Don't make trying to find an 800 number on your web site like a game of "Where's Waldo?" Plenty of customers have a good reason for wanting to contact you via phone versus sending e-mail or visiting your frequently asked questions (FAQ) page—either they can't find answers to their questions using those resources or they need more detailed and nuanced responses than those avenues provide. List your 800 number boldly on every Web page.

5. *Monitor the Online Buzz.* More companies are listening to their customers by monitoring online discussion boards, chat rooms, and blogs to stay on top of what's being said about their products or services. While they know they can't control online word of mouth, and many of the rants may be un-

founded, they nonetheless see it as valuable market research tool. If companies come across a critical mass of complaints about some aspect of their performance, it may be a sign they need to follow up. Monitoring online commentary also can be a useful way of picking up new ideas for improving service, since offering such suggestions is one of the favorite pastimes of bloggers and users of online discussions boards.

6. *Customer Advisory Panels.* Your best customers, the ones who have been with you for years, represent not only a valued relationship but a source of savvy insight into your service operations. Use them like a board of directors for the front line. Your worst can also be an asset when you find active ways to listen. Emerald Peoples Utility District, a small public power co-op based in Eugene, Oregon, gets customers involved in various committees and study groups. Arizona Public Service (APS), a much larger regional utility based in Phoenix, Arizona has recruited some of the public interest advocates who once dogged its every step to bring their interest and energy inside the walls, where they can be applied in useful ways. Retailers have been known to use panels of customers to help them anticipate fashion trends, and electronics companies often tap knowledgeable customers for feedback on design, standards, and pricing of their products.

## The Power of Formal Research

Last, but certainly not least, there's the spectrum of more formal techniques for data collection. Mail-in, Web-based, and live surveys, focus groups, telemarketing contacts, mystery shopping services, demographic analysis, and random sampling of target audiences all help shade in the various colors of the big picture.

1. *Customer Surveys.* Face-to-face, via e-mail, snail mail, on Web sites or over the telephone (or through a combination), ask customers to rate you on overall satisfaction or "delight," on the success of the last transaction they had with you, on

specific aspects of your service delivery system, and perhaps most important, on how likely they'd be to recommend you to colleagues or friends. The latter question measures how well you've done at creating "passionate promoters" of your company. Then feed the results back into your system.

Be sure to ask both importance and performance questions. Measuring the two dimensions helps ensure you're assessing things that really matter to customers, not just factors that market researchers assume have the biggest influence on repurchase intentions or satisfaction levels. The approach will help you avoid spending dollars on fixing things—or adding amenities—that have little impact on customer loyalty.

2. *Focus Groups.* Bringing current customers together to discuss the good, the bad, and the ugly of what you do puts flesh on the bones of survey data. Customers can problem-solve with you, rate and rank the relative importance of different aspects of your service (the Moments of Truth that define the shape and style of your services in customers' eyes), and explain how different elements of a transaction affect their perceptions of you. Employee focus groups work as well as customer focus groups. Bring a group of employees together and ask such questions as "What are our customers saying to you?" and "What gets in your way of delivering good service?" and "What can we do to help keep you fresh and renewed so you can better handle the challenge of dealing with customers all day?"

3. *Employee Visit Teams.* Send teams of front-line workers, supervisors, and support people out to look at the customers' "points of contact" (with you and your competitors) from the customers' point of view. Their assignment: Bring back ideas for improving transactional quality based on customer experiences. What are the pluses and minuses of your service delivery system versus alternative systems when seen in this light?

4. *Mystery Shopping Services.* Some companies specialize in playing the role of customer and giving feedback on your customer contact performance. The best ones work with

you to develop checklists or evaluation scales based on your service vision statement; some will even put their people through your service training so they know exactly how your people are supposed to be doing things. As a twist, you can use your own employees as shoppers as well. It is also possible to do comparison shopping of your competition using your own criteria for good service.

5. *Toll-Free Hotlines.* A good service recovery system almost always has a hotline of some sort, with service employees trained and focused on resolving customer problems on first contact. Many customer-centric companies create toll-free lines for specific product or service offerings, and others have gone multilingual—Federal Express, for example, has an interactive voice response system that allows customers to speak to English or Spanish customer service personnel. Customers who call in to register a complaint, make a suggestion, ask a question, or have a problem solved offer extremely valuable input on your service delivery system.

The key to making a toll-free number work is data capture and analysis. It is more difficult than it sounds to get people in Department A to work with people in Department B on service systems improvement. This is especially true when one of the departments is seen as the "complaint handling specialists." Incentives are usually needed. And objectives. And attention to detail.

6. *Benchmarking.* Started as a way to compare operational efficiencies with companies that have similar problems or challenges but aren't in your business (so data can be shared without concern for competitive consequences), benchmarking has become more broadly defined today as a way of looking for breakthrough ideas by seeing how others are seeing their customers. The original purpose of benchmarking related directly to improving a service delivery system by comparing operational ideas and numbers with a world class company in another industry. That is still the best use possible, but don't overlook the teaching examples provided by any organization's comparative experiences.

Listening is useless unless it creates actions which realign efforts based on what is learned.

—Fred Smith
Founder and Chairman
FedEx

# 6

# A Complaining Customer Is Your Best Friend

One of the surest signs of a bad or declining relationship with a customer is the absence of complaints. Nobody is ever that satisfied, especially not over an extended period of time. The customer is either not being candid or not being contacted.

—Theodore Levitt
Business School Professor, Harvard University

As a manager it can be easy to subscribe to "no news is good news" thinking when it comes to your staff's service performance. You work diligently to ensure your people have the right training, coaching, and technology to give customers their best every day, and you see firsthand much of the good work they do to solve vexing problems and address tough questions. When customer satisfaction reports turn up only a handful of formal complaints, it's natural and comforting to believe those numbers reflect the bang-up job your staff has done at creating a critical mass of happy customers.

But experts at TARP Worldwide, an Arlington, Virginia-based customer service research firm, will tell you it's also the kind of thinking that can prove dangerous to the health of your organization's bottom line. TARP research finds that only 50 percent of customers with serious problems ever bother to complain, and more than 90 percent of customers with smaller problems never take the time to say anything about it. What these upset customers do instead of contacting the offending company, of course, is silently slip away to the competition, never to donate to your corporate coffers again. The truth is that most unhappy customers would rather switch than fight, usually because they don't like confrontation or are convinced their complaints will result in little substantive change.

## The Trouble with Customer Silence

When it comes to customer relationships silence isn't golden. The reality is things often go wrong over the course of a service relationship, and when they do you want to know about it, and the sooner the better. At least, you do if you're sincerely interested in building a long-term relationship that's strong enough to weather the occasional goof or glitch. Too often we encounter managers who, when presented with bad news, revert to playground behaviors and hum loudly or cover their ears to avoid having to hear it.

In a way, as legendary Harvard marketing professor Theodore Levitt once observed, a quality customer relationship is like a marriage. "The sale consummates the courtship," he writes, "at which point the marriage begins. The quality of the 'marriage' depends on how well the seller manages the relationship."

Just as personal relationships have their occasional rough spots, so too will a customer relationship have its ups and downs. If there's real long-term value in the relationship, both parties will have an incentive to overcome the periodic problems and, through the process of doing so, make the relationship even stronger. In contrast, an absence of candor that causes one partner to gloss over or fail to mention problems reflects declining trust and a deteriorating relationship.

A strong, enduring customer service relationship will be founded on clear, open communications—whether the matter at hand is good or bad. Customers who take the time to bring their problems to us or offer advice on how we can better meet their needs are customers who believe we care enough to act on their complaints, not just feel good about their compliments. They're telling us they still see value in the relationship continuing—if, that is, things can get back to a sound and mutually satisfying level.

Wise companies view customer complaints as the pearl inside the oyster. The fact is that customers who complain can become even *more* loyal to your company than those who experience no problems with you at all ... if their complaints are handled in an effective and rapid manner. Research by Marriott Hotels, for example, found that for customers who had experienced some problems during their stay but had those issues satisfactorily resolved before they left the hotel, 94 percent said they would use the hotel again. However, 89 percent of customers who had experienced *no* problems during their stay said they intended to come back to the Marriott again.

By contrast, avoiding complaints, pretending that everything is "just peachy" (even when you know it isn't), pretending to assertively solicit customer feedback with one hand while backhanding the customer for daring to utter a discouraging word with the other are sure signs that the relationship has not achieved enough maturity to weather the candor. That way lies dissolution. Since in the event of divorce, a valued customer always gets custody of the "business" they bring to a relationship, you'll not only have to replace them, you'll also have to watch them take up with your bitterest rivals: your competition.

## Stimulating Complaints

While it might be counterintuitive to think that people who've been wronged—seriously or otherwise—would hesitate to complain about the perceived injustice, research sheds light on why customers often choose "flight over fight."

Consider, for example, why an upset diner usually answers "fine" if asked how everything was, when, in fact, the meal and/or the service were a disappointment? Or why customers often wear clothes and shoes that are half a size too large or too small rather than return them to the store for a replacement that fits better? Don't these customers know how much we want and need their feedback today?

In point of fact, they don't know. There are three basic reasons why customers choose to vote with their feet and go looking for another service provider rather than stick around and try to work the problem through with us:

1. They don't think we care.
2. They don't have any hope for a satisfactory resolution to their problem—they don't think anything good is going to happen, even if we do care.
3. They don't have any courage—experience has taught them that "no good turn goes unpunished," leading them to fear that the service provider will find a way to retaliate against them the next time.

Together these beliefs create what's known as "trained hopelessness." Customers don't complain because they feel there's little chance that speaking up will spur real change or trigger a prompt, satisfactory response.

Though customers are not inclined to tell us, it's worth noting that they will tell plenty of other people: 14 to 20 of them on average when they're not happy, according to TARP data. That means you've transformed plenty of upset customers into evangelists who gleefully spread the word about their unsavory experience not only in face-to-face encounters, but to all corners of the globe courtesy of blogs, online discussion boards, chat rooms, and e-mail. If the data on how many people aggrieved customers tell about their bad experiences at cocktail parties or on coffee breaks isn't enough to get your attention, the fact that bad news now travels at light speed via the Internet should certainly make you sit up and pay heed.

Comparatively speaking, truly satisfied customers will tell just five to seven people about a service provider who really dazzled them. And what do researchers consistently find to be the most powerful and persuasive form of advertising? You guessed it—word of mouth.

## Warts and All

Over the years, businesses have done a pretty fair job of convincing customers to suffer in silence. Now, when we want this kind of informed feedback, we have to literally coax customers to provide it. There are a lot of reasons for this state of affairs:

- In some cases, we've lulled ourselves into thinking no news is good news, or that it's better to "let sleeping dogs lie."
- Sometimes we fear that if we seek and receive customer complaints, and no corrective action ensues, we might be perceived in a worse light than if we'd left well enough alone. Research, however, contradicts that assumption: *Better to have asked and not acted, it finds, than not to have asked at all.*
- In some cases, we simply haven't figured out how to effectively ask for complaints without sounding almost masochistic: "Please, tell us how bad we are."
- When customers do take the time to complain, but jaded or indifferent front-line employees discount the complaint as "we hear a lot of that" or "that tends to happen quite a bit here towards the end of the quarter," customers feel their complaints aren't taken seriously and are hesitant to speak up again. If it happens enough, they'll simply pull up stakes for greener pastures.

## How to Make Complaining Easier

Complaining customers are important in and of themselves. Their relationship with us is in obvious jeopardy and needs to be returned to a positive state. Complaining customers also are important because, statistically speaking, they represent other dissatisfied customers who are convinced that there's no point in telling us about their bad experiences with us. These customers are saying, "Please don't throw us away. We want the opportunity to be your customer again." Following are some tactics to help you get the most from those encounters.

1. *When you have an opportunity to address a complainant face-to-face, listen.* Work consciously at graciousness and control. Avoid becoming defensive or acting stern and cold or judgmental. Especially avoid attempting to explain why the problem occurred. When they are levying complaints, customers are not particularly interested in your explanations for poor service, let alone what *they* should have done differently. They want to know: (1) that they are being heard, and (2) that their comments are valued. Your explanations of why things work the way they do ("I'm just stating our policy") will be seen as defensive and will only aggravate and irritate.

2. *Treat complaints about your customer contact people as an opportunity.* Use them for problem-solving and learning, not for rebuke and judgment. If you punish your front-line people when they bring you customer complaints or feedback, they will find ways to keep future feedback from you. *Keep in mind that the customer is not always right.* Research shows that about 30 percent of all service problems are actually caused by the customer; they fail to read user manuals or other important literature they're sent, plead ignorance about refund policies, ask you to share proprietary information about competitors, or simply make unreasonable requests. The objective isn't to assign blame and hand out punishment. It's to find out what happened, why, what you can do to resolve it this time and what you can do to prevent it from happening again.

3. *Be assertive in soliciting customer feedback.* Nothing you or your people are doing is more important than taking care of customers. That process doesn't end with ringing up a sale. Stimulate the dialogue with words like "We are really eager to do all we can to improve our service, and your feedback would be very helpful." Don't shut the door on additional details, either. When they've gotten through the key points of the

story, probe for helpful details and other ideas: "Thanks, that helps a lot. What else could we do to improve our service?"

4. *Encourage your front-line people to ask for feedback.* Make it clear by words and actions that you think customers can help you build rewarding, long-term, profitable relationships that benefit everyone involved. Be a good role model by asking customers for feedback in the presence of your front-line staff. Listen, understand, and respond to what your staffers have been hearing so they know that you'll act on what they can tell you.

5. *Use negative feedback to improve performance, not punish people.* When you get complaints from customers regarding your people, thank the customer involved for the information and make it clear that you will check into the problem, but without either scapegoating your employees or "shooting the messenger" by defending your people on general principles. Then, when you meet with your front-line person, present the feedback, not in a blaming or judgmental way, but with a descriptive "Let's figure out what we can do to resolve this situation" type of approach.

6. *Don't take sides.* If you find yourself in the line of fire between the customer and your employee, take the high ground. Instead of choosing sides, your best approach will be to try to collect facts and make a decision based on the *performance*, not the *people* involved. Remember that win-lose situations leave losers (and negative feelings) in their aftermath. Your goal should be to strike a balance between reaffirming the customer for complaining and reinforcing your people so they'll continue to have the confidence to deal with customers.

> Your most unhappy customers are your greatest source of learning.
>
> —Bill Gates
> Chairman, Microsoft Corporation

# 7

# The Binding Power of Customer Trust

When people honor each other, there is a trust established that leads to synergy, interdependence and
deep respect. Both parties make decisions and
choices based on what is right, what is best, and what
is valued most highly.

—Blaine Lee
Founding Vice President
Covey Leadership Center

Trust is the platinum standard of customer service, the glue that keeps customers coming back again and again. Peoples' faith in your word and your promises is what separates you from organizations that don't have clients' best interests at heart and would sooner save a dime than ensure customers walk away from transactions feeling honored and respected.

Customer trust grows slowly and develops over time by a succession of positive experiences. But it can be dashed by a single incident of unfaithfulness or cemented by a solitary memorable act.

Fairness is one of customers' most critical trust-creating hot buttons. Treat people unfairly—from their point of view— and risk losing them forever as clients. Treat them with high regard and even-handedness and you'll quickly set yourself apart from the mass of organizations customers view with a wary eye. Call it the "protective big brother" effect. When customers feel an organization is looking out for them, it creates a powerful bond—a transactional blood tie—that becomes difficult to break.

What is fairness from the customer's viewpoint? That can and does often vary from customer to customer. But in general, our research shows customers feel treated fairly when:

- You keep the promises you make.
- You acknowledge their unique needs and wishes.
- You place their best interests ahead of the company's standard operating procedures.
- You are candid and don't resort to "spin" in explaining why a problem occurred, and you apologize if the organization is at fault.
- You make the process of achieving a satisfactory outcome painless, not akin to hand-to-hand combat with the enemy.

## Customer Trust Breeds Loyalty

Christopher Hart, president of the Spire Group in Brookline, Massachusetts and a former faculty member at Harvard and the University of Michigan, has labeled the "explosion of positive affective feelings" that lead to strong levels of customer loyalty and repeat business the "Total-Trust Platform." As Hart explains it, total trust goes beyond the realm of customer satisfaction to creating a feeling among customers that a company will act in their best interests. Customer trust is the belief, backed by repeated experiences with an organization, that employees will be fair, reliable, and ethical in all of their dealings with customers.

Is Total-Trust simply an idealistic academic musing or is there substance behind the glowing rhetoric? Hart suggests that there are plenty of companies that have long inspired such confidence in their customers. Among the names on his short list: FedEx, Intuit, USAA, Lands' End, and Johnson & Johnson. Perfect companies? By no means, but Hart insists when they fail, they do so by error of *omission* versus *commission*. Explains Hart: "It's like a marriage. You can forget an important occasion or fight with your spouse and still have a trusting relationship. However, if you get caught cheating, that can destroy the relationship."

When a car repair shop neglects to tell you that your needed repair far exceeded the original estimate, a cell phone provider regularly overcharges you on billing statements despite repeated complaints about the problem, or a retailer doesn't honor its advertised return policy or service guarantee, it becomes tantamount to cheating on the relationship.

## Candor and Communication Build Trust

Trust is sown through the small acts of communication and caring that make customers feel like you're on their team, not playing for the opposition. When the mechanic or service manager takes time to explain all of your car repair options—from the cheaper quick fix to the more expensive long-term solution, without trying to cross-sell you on a litany of other repairs they "just happened to discover in a routine inspection" while under the hood—it engenders a sense of trust. When the pilot candidly explains why your plane has sat on the runway 30 minutes past its scheduled departure time—rather than leaving you sitting in the dark, wondering if there's been a terrorist incident—it begins to create trust. When the front desk clerk at the hotel overhears you telling your wife about your pounding headache, then sends some complimentary aspirin up to your room, that is a trust-building moment.

Creating trust takes on heightened importance in the world of e-commerce, where customers can't take products for test-drives, look salespeople in the eye, or be won over by a gleaming headquarters building. They need to trust that you'll protect their data privacy—a growing concern with identify theft and "cyber crime" on the rise—and that you'll send ordered product on time and in good condition. Second chances are rare in the online world. Send the first order a customer places to your Web site well beyond the promised delivery date, or have it arrive with damaged or missing parts, or make the hassle factor high if they try to return it, and it's unlikely they'll give you a "make-up" opportunity.

## Trust-Creating Exemplars

Progressive Insurance is one company that walks the trust-building talk. In 2002 the Ohio-based company began scrolling car insurance rates for its competitors across the home page of its Web site—along with its own rates, even when they were higher. *Fast Company* magazine was so impressed by the practice, along with other of the insurer's service strategies, that it gave Progressive one of its "Customer First" awards in 2004. "Imagine walking into a Circuit City prepared to buy a digital camera and being told you could get it cheaper at Best Buy," wrote the magazine's editors. "Sound crazy? If a customer shopping for car insurance calls Progressive, that's pretty much what happens."

While the company undoubtedly loses customers because of the practice, CEO Glenn Renwick believes the transparency keeps a far larger number loyal to the organization. "We hope it establishes a feeling of trust for the company," he told the magazine.

Progressive's trust-building efforts go beyond providing competitor's rates. When customers are involved in accidents, the company sends out immediate response vehicles (IRVs) to the accident site or client homes to assess the damage, and in many cases they pay out claims on the spot. Progressive says the vehicles are designed in part to deal with distressed customers' "emotional EKGs" following accidents. Some IRVs even have been known to beat police or emergency vehicles to the scene of accidents involving Progressive clients.

Trust also is built by sales practices that work to match products or services to customers' unique needs, not try to "fit a prospect to a presentation" or force-feed clients things that aren't in their best interests. Low-pressure sales approaches can ratchet up customer trust levels. When customers approach the makeup counter of Kiehl's, the New York-based chain of drugstores, they are encouraged to take free samples of lipstick or skin products and try them out before they ever buy; each year the store gives away millions of such goodwill-generating samples.

It's all part of Kiehls' trust-engendering sales approach, which teaches associates to avoid making promises they can't keep and never to make customers feel like they're getting the hard sell.[1] Trusting organizations put more focus on nurturing relationships and encouraging repeat business than squeezing every dollar out of every transaction. This doesn't mean "giving away the shop"; employees should always be encouraged to protect and grow the assets of the organization. But customers remember organizations that refrain from "nickel and diming them to death."

Product return and repair policies present another golden opportunity to build trust. When a customer has a problem with a computer purchased at Dell Computer, the company often sends the customer a replacement, a program to transfer files from the old to the new computer, and mailing labels to send back the defective machine. How many organizations might manage the return process the other way around—"Send us the computer and then we'll . . .?" Winning organizations bet on the long-term relationship and demonstrate trust for customers. When an organization takes a risk with customers, customers usually respond in kind . . . and their loyalty soars.

How solid is your organization's Trust Platform? Ask your customers the following questions—if you dare:

- Do you believe our company would knowingly sell you a product or service you do not need?
- If we were able to reduce our operating costs, do you believe we would pass some of the savings along to customers?
- If we could raise our prices without you noticing, do you believe we would?

## Trust and Service Recovery

The essence of the psychological side of recovery—getting things returned to normal for customers following a problem—is restoring trust, or the customer's belief that you will keep the explicit and implicit promises you made. Dr. Kathleen Seiders, an associate professor of marketing at

[1]Jennifer Vilaga, "Profitable Player: Kiehl's," *Fast Company,* October 2005.

Boston College says that trust is particularly at risk when the customer feels vulnerable; that is, they perceive that all the power to set things right is in the organization's hands and little or nothing is under their control. That sense of vulnerability is highest when the customer feels he or she lacks:

*Information:* They are left in the dark about what is going on, or how long it might take to set things right.

*Expertise:* The customer himself couldn't fix the car or the computer hard drive or the fouled-up reservation on a bet. All of the "smarts" are on your side.

*Freedom:* There is no other option for fixing the problem aside from dealing with you. The customer perceives you as their only hope. Customers may be free contractually to ask someone else to solve the problem, but there is no one else, or at least they see it that way.

Restoring trust in recovery situations is a multistep process. The first step requires involving customers in problem resolution—"tell me again exactly what was happening when the mower stopping running?" or "can you give me a rundown on the history of this problem?" then reassuring the customer that the problem is fixable. Then you need to deliver on your promise. If you perform all three steps well and apologize for the problem and empathize effectively, you will cement customer trust and have them coming back for more.

If you sincerely want that bond of trust with your customers, every action of every employee, top to bottom—starting and ending with yours—has to pass the trust test. You have to demonstrate trust in your customers if you want and need them to trust you. You get back what you give. It works that way with your employees, your peers, your family, and your friends. And it definitely works that way with your customers.

> You may be deceived if you trust too much, but you will live in torment if you don't trust enough.
>
> —Frank Crane
> Presbyterian Minister
> Author *Four Minute Essays*

# 8

# Little Things
# Mean a Lot

It's not the one thousand dollar things that upset the
customer, but the five buck things that bug them.
—Earl Fletcher
Sales and Management Trainer
Volkswagen Canada

New arrivals to the combat zones of Vietnam quickly learned
that the difference between a veteran and a novice was far
more than war stories. They had an expression for it on the
front lines: "grunt eyes." Grunts were the enlisted ranks of the
infantry—low rank, little prestige, people whose job description started and ended with the simple requirement, "Do what
the 'old man' tells you to do."

Those with "grunt eyes" were able to see things a new in-
country recruit would completely miss. And there was little
correlation with rank. Whether you were a captain or a private, you only acquired "grunt eyes" in the field, paying attention to every sight, sound, smell, impulse, clue, and condition that often could make the difference between life and
death. It was something learned, not something taught. The
common skeptic's question, immortalized in the movie *Full
Metal Jacket* was "I see you talk the talk, but do you walk the
walk?"

As a manager, you've no doubt learned a fair amount of service talk in recent years. But have you also learned the service walk? Have you developed "grunt eyes" attuned to your own front-line conditions? Do you really notice and understand the subtleties of what you see? The survival of your business is riding on it. According to our survey research, about 22 percent of the difference between passionate and dispassionate customers can be accounted for by an organization's ability to recognize and manage the details that really matter for customers.

Attention to details is a prime characteristic of Knock Your Socks Off Service.

Fred Smith, founder and chairman of FedEx, begins many of his visits in various FedEx cities by hopping into a delivery van and riding with a driver to see his operations where they most affect the customer.

Bill Marriott, chairman of the hotel chain that bears the family name, often takes a turn at the front desk checking in guests. If he sees a dirty ashtray in the lobby, he empties it. If there is trash in the parking lot, he picks it up.

Similarly, grunt-eyed managers and front liners alike at Walt Disney World and Disneyland, Chick-fil-A restaurants, Starbucks, Lexus dealerships, Romano's Macaroni Grills, and thousands of other dedicated businesses pick up trash, polish counters, straighten displays, spruce up plants, and worry over the 101 details that together combine to make their customers' experiences with them memorable for all the right reasons.

Managers in these organizations know that it's the little service problems—small scale neglect—that often lead to bigger ones. It's a belief that mirrors the "broken windows" theory on how to control crime first expounded by sociologists James Wilson and George Kelling in an *Atlantic Monthly* article. A broken window, graffiti-scarred building, littered sidewalk, or abandoned building does no great harm to a neighborhood if promptly fixed. However, if they are left unaddressed, it sends a signal to criminals that no one cares about the neighborhood and encourages them to break in, vandalize, deal drugs, and more. Soon more serious crimes like burglary, robbery, rape, and even murder begin to occur. Mayor Rudy Guiliani used the philosophy to great effect to clean up large parts of New York City. The corollary for the business world? When the details are overlooked and little things are left to fester, it can breed indifference and sloppiness on a larger level among service staff.

Attention to details involves more than just playing janitor so your people will know they should imitate your concern for what the customer sees. It also means remembering that details are at the heart of the Moments of Truth, those moments when the customer is in contact with your organization and forms an opinion of the quality of what you do. At Romano's Macaroni Grill, every general manager is expected to do the "little thing" of greeting and talking to customers to ensure they enjoy their visits. To Vic Pisano, the general manager of the original Macaroni grill, simply showing you care about guests can go a long way toward creating repeat business. "You welcome everyone who comes in the door, you make sure the food is good, and you make sure the people you serve are happy," he says. The only way to do that, Pisano says, is by visiting tables and talking to customers.[1]

Manage the Moments of Truth well and you earn an A or a B on customers' highly subjective report cards. Ignore them, or manage them poorly, and customers give you a D or an F. Then they start looking for someone more likely to make the grade.

## The Service Walk

Every customer typically goes through many, many moments of truth to get a particular need met. As mentioned earlier, a moment of truth is any encounter a customer has in which he or she has an opportunity to give the organization a thumb's up or down. However, it's not easy to figure out which of the hundreds of moments of truth customers experience might be

---

[1]Ron Zemke and Chip Bell, *Service Magic: The Art of Amazing Your Customers* (Dearborn, MI: Dearborn Financial Publishing, 2003), p. 165.

*deal breakers*—interactions where the quality of service rendered has an inordinate influence on whether they decide to keep doing business with you—and which have a lesser effect on their repurchase intentions. Traditional measurement and analysis can help you zero in on customer priorities: both the large-scale kind, such as market research and detailed customer surveys, and more anecdotal and fragmented forms, like customer comment cards, surveys attached to e-mail, phone calls, and impromptu conversations with customers you meet on and off the job.

Not all moments of truth are created equal in the eyes of customers. In other words, before you make your people crazy by mandating that telephones will be answered within two rings, make sure your customers consider that an important service quality factor. What impact does a quick answer have on overall satisfaction or customers' decisions to keep doing business with you? Or how about mandating that employees say "hello" to each and every customer that enters a retail business? While management might see these as vital service dimensions, customers often view it differently. View other details from the customer's standpoint as well. It will save you a lot of headaches and resources spent on making improvements that have little or no effect on customer loyalty.

Defining the details in general is only a starting point. You can't manage service in absentia. You need to develop your own "grunt eyes" when it comes to service, making sure you walk the walk as well as talk the talk.

To take the "service walk," start by determining how your services look to your customers based on their prepurchase expectations. When you enter a bank or a car repair shop, a theater or a fast-food restaurant, a doctor's office or an airplane, you have some notion of what ought to occur. The first thing you do is compare what's actually happening to that expectation. And when it doesn't match up, you can find yourself disoriented and confused—whether because you're dismayed or dazzled.

- If you walked into a Subway, Chick-fil-A or McDonald's and found candles and fine china on the tables, with

waiters in tuxedos hovering nearby, you'd think you were in the wrong place—or in the middle of a *Saturday Night Live* skit.
- By the same token, if you arrived for dinner at five-star Chez Ritzy and encountered the standard Subway or McDonald's decor, menu, and service style, you would also wonder what was afoot.

From that starting point, service quality becomes a function of experience—what happens to you as the customer. That's why it's so important to see and evaluate your services the way your clients do. The math involved is relatively simple. If the experience matches their expectations, they'll judge it to be satisfactory, though hardly memorable. When it turns out differently than they expected, it becomes more memorable precisely because of its lower or higher than expected quality.

Two factors are considered by the customer: process and outcome—what they experience and what they get. Both must match expectations for service to be judged satisfactory; both must exceed expectations for service to be viewed as superior. But if either is substandard, the customer's combined rating will drop off the bottom of the charts.

- When the meal (outcome) is wonderful, but you have to go through hell (process) to get it—waiting forever for your meal or arriving home to find items missing from a drive-through order—the net score will be negative.
- Likewise, even when you're treated like a king by the car repair shop (process), if your car still doesn't work properly (outcome), the net score is negative. In other words, an incompetent physical administered by a personable and humorous doctor will not satisfy. However, neither will a competent physical administered by a brusque, arrogant physician—or one who hasn't bathed since the last full moon. Ditto for a cheery and courteous customer service rep who places you on hold numerous times to consult with coworkers, then eventually disconnects you, in a well-mean-

ing but bumbling attempt to answer a question he should be able to quickly address on his own.

The caring is as important as the care to winning the customer's loyalty. You have to do both to succeed.

## Dealing with Details

Many organizations put a great deal of time and energy into managing and monitoring the service outcome—the check was cashed, the operation was completed, the account was closed. Outcomes, by and large, are easy to define and count. But paying attention to all the little details involved in the service process is a lot tougher. It's difficult to identify and define, let alone measure and evaluate, everything the customer has to go through to get to that outcome. But that's what you, and everyone working with and for you, must learn to do as part of your service walk.

To see just how detailed your customer-level journey can be, consider the variables involved only at the points where a customer might enter your delivery system in these various settings:

• *A Parking Lot.* Is it easy to access, well lit, clearly marked, safe to use? Are the parking lot's users (customers) favored over the parking lot's owners (your people, especially internal VIPs)? Is it clear from wherever the customers have to park which door should be entered? Ask yourself, "If the customer's experience in the parking lot were a picture of our whole service system, what would it tell them about what we value, how we feel about customers, where our priorities lie?"

• *An Admitting Office, a Reception Area, or a Security Check-In.* How is the area kept? Is it comfortable, clean, user-friendly? Is it easy for customers to figure out where to go, who to see, what to do? Are there resources, aids, supports, and guides if the customer gets confused, bored, or lost? Are such materials current and professional, or does their age qualify them as museum pieces? What is done to manage wait time?

What would a picture of this scene tell the customer about the rest of the service delivery systems they'll shortly be encountering?

• *Objects, Forms, Web Sites, Systems, or Procedures.* Are they clearly written, professionally produced, easily navigated, truly necessary? Will they be perceived as user-friendly and customer-focused, or confusing and awkwardly designed? Can instructions or procedures be understood by the customer without the aid of a dictionary, an interpreter, or an information technology guru? The most precious commodity for many customers today is time—and if you waste it with a confusing Web site design or cumbersome administrative procedures, they probably won't return for more punishment.

• *Inbound Call Center.* Is the system large enough and sophisticated enough to handle the call load, easy to understand and use, efficient and time-effective? Must your customers negotiate their way through a long and involved voice mail system made up of seemingly endless menus of buttons to push before encountering a live human voice? Are phone encounters rushed to meet an artificial time standard? Or prolonged well beyond the time the customer has allotted for your assistance due to poor staff training or a bored service rep's desire for chit chat? If the customer must be transferred, how will it feel and sound on their end of the line? What do they experience when they're put on hold—silence, elevator music, boring advertisements, long waits?

## Service Patrols

The service walk can be taken solo, but it's an equally valid tactic as something you do with one or several of your frontline people. From time to time, ask some of *them* to join you in trying on the customer's clodhoppers. Let them tell you what they see when they use their own "grunt eyes" to reexamine aspects of the service delivery system and experience that have become taken for granted over time. Ask them to point out weak spots, bottlenecks, points of pride and embarrassment, and areas for improvement identified by customers and their own firsthand knowledge of what is involved in taking care of business.

If it's not practical to get them to accompany you, ask them to sample your service on their own. Have them critique how user-friendly your Web site is or how easy it is to access the options they need (including live help) on your voice mail system. Asking for your staff's input has the added benefit of making them feel more valued and respected.

The more you encourage front-line people to see themselves as responsible for the service experience—and the systems that make those experiences successful or difficult—the more willing and empowered they will feel to truly take care of their customers.

Jan Carlzon, architect of the well-documented service turnaround at Scandinavian Airline Systems (SAS), once summarized the journey from hip-deep red ink to basic black on the bottom line as a matter of details, details, details: "We never started out to become 1,000 percent better at anything; just 1 percent better at a thousand different things that are important to the customer—and it worked."

But at SAS, just as at Progressive Insurance, Zappos Shoes, Best Buy, Southwest Airlines, W Hotels, UPS, and countless other outstanding service providers, managers continue to not only talk the talk, but walk the walk.

> You don't improve service and quality in general.
> You improve service and quality in specific.
>
> —Dr. Rodney Dueck
> Park Nicollet Medical Centers
> Minneapolis, Minnesota

# Imperative 3
# Build a Service Vision

Yogi Berra, the immortal New York Yankee catcher and coach, is supposed to have said, "If you don't know where you're going, you're liable to end up someplace else." It's true—whether he said it or not. It is especially true of your efforts to create Knock Your Socks Off Service. Your vision of what superior service looks like is the foundation of getting where you want to go. And not "someplace else."

Focusing on *purpose* means articulating that vision for the people who work with you. What it will take to cause customers to give you a five-star rating may be very clear in *your* mind. That is of little consequence until everyone charged with turning that vision into reality for the customer sees that vision just as clearly as you.

That vision—we refer to it as a "service strategy statement"—must be personally meaningful and important to everyone in the organization if it is going to become reality for the customer. That means it must not only be understandable, it must also be measurable. Concrete standards of service quality make the vision real and palpable; regular and extensive measurement makes it meaningful.

# 9

# The Power of Purpose

Employees shouldn't be expected to deliver first-rate service if management can't first define it.
—Horst Schulze
Retired President of the Ritz-Carlton
Hotel Company

A cattle rancher will tell you that moving a large herd requires bifocal vision: without close attention to the herd, a feisty steer can double back or break away, making the rancher waste important time retrieving the malcontent. But if you don't also keep an eye on the distant gate—your ultimate destination—you may never funnel the herd through it.

When it comes to Knock Your Socks Off Service, focusing on the ultimate and the immediate is equally critical. "Bifocal" service vision comes from a clear focus on purpose: Defining in detail and in writing—and then repeating constantly and consistently—what your organization means when it says "Quality customer service is our goal." Your focus on purpose—your service *vision*— is your tool for aligning the day-to-day actions of your employees with the distant gate of Knock Your Socks Off Service.

Your organization probably has a mission statement. That's great. But to keep your unit focus sharp, you need your own well-defined, carefully worded service *vision* statement. Your statement may be unique to your unit or a variation on the organization's central strategy. It should contain a profile of your core customer base, describe what you do that is of value to them, and explain how you—and they—will know it when your goal of customer delight is achieved. It should also clarify the aspects of your service approach that separate you from competitors in customers' eyes.

Customers relish consistency. Texas A & M researcher Leonard Berry and colleagues found that the number one attribute customers value in the service they receive is *reliability*—your ability to provide what was promised, dependably and accurately. Customers want the service from branch A to be as good as branch B; they don't like having to choose a specific location—or a specific teller, floor salesperson, or waiter—because opting for others represents a roll of the dice. We want them all to be effective. How do you get everyone in the organization "rowing together as one" to deliver a consistently high level of service? It starts with a compelling and actionable service vision.

Defining what you are trying to ultimately accomplish with and for customers helps your people understand the rhyme and reason of the work they do. Your vision statement should be so well defined that your people always know which side to come down on when they face decisions about how to provide truly superior service. It's not magic. It's simply the power of purpose.

Your service vision statement, when done well, will:

- Ensure that everyone in your unit is working with the same idea of "what's important around here."
- Act as the "lens" through which front-liners view every decision they make or action they take that impacts customers.
- Help individual employees understand the rationale behind organizational policy so they have confidence in resolving unique and unusual situations.
- Serve as the foundation for service standards, norms and metrics.
- Describe what makes your approach to service distinct in the marketplace.
- Provide a tool for aligning strategy and effort so customers enjoy consistency and reliability in service quality.

Here's what our research has found about the "power of purpose" in creating Knock Your Socks Off Service:

- If you do not have a definition of what good service means, your chances of getting high marks from your customers are about three in 10.
- If you have a very general definition, your chances of getting high marks from your customers improve to about 50-50.
- If you have a detailed definition of what good service means—if it is defined in the context of the *company* and the *customer*, if it is well communicated to employees, and tied to specific standards and measures— your chances of getting high marks from your customers are close to 90 percent.

## Helping Employees Focus

A service vision statement isn't something simply to hang on the wall or pass out on laminated wallet cards. Once it exists, there are a multitude of ways to give it life and power.

- *Test decisions against your service vision.* Enlist one, two, perhaps even all of your employees to give you feedback on the consistency between your actions and the vision statement. And thank them for their help!
- *Ask front liners to use it to evaluate your unit's policies, procedures, and general "ways of doing things."* Are they consistent with the vision? Do they really help get things done for the customers? If not, where do they interfere with giving good service? And how can they be changed?
- *Hold "what's stupid around here?" meetings.* Use the vision statement to help identify outmoded practices, time-wasters, repeated trouble spots, and customer-vexing aspects of your business that make you look dumb to your customers—and each other.

• *Set "stop, start, and measure" objectives.* Perhaps once a quarter, ask every employee to come with a list of items under three headings:

1. Things we should stop doing around here.
2. Things we should start doing around here.
3. Things we don't track or measure—but should.

• *Hold a "focus fantasy" meeting with your employees.* Ask your people to discuss who they would like to be like: If they could model the business in general and their behaviors in particular after a famous or respected organization, who would it be and why? Universal Orlando? QVC? Container Store? Home Depot? Lexus? Their neighborhood grocer or hardware store? Or discuss what you would have to do differently to make the cover of the leading trade journal in your industry. Then act on what you hear.

The power of purpose is the power of knowing what to do, and when and how to do it, without having to be told. It helps your people take control of their work and frees them from the adolescent dependence on "management" that characterizes too many businesses today. It allows you to stop acting like a parent and start working with your people as adults.

If you use your service vision as a lens through which to look from the inside out, you should see the things customers value and that can set your organization apart. If you use it as a lens to look from the outside in, you should get a consistent service focus that helps your people to work in "sync"—their actions in alignment with strategic goals.

> If you don't know where you are going, any road will take you there.

> —David Campbell
> Industrial Psychologist

# 10

# Getting Your Vision Down on Paper

Vision without action is dreaming. Action without vision is random activity. Vision and action together can change the world.

—Joel Barker
Futurist

A good service vision statement involves customers and employees. It takes on tangible shape and form when you actually put it on paper where everyone can see and use it. As you work to define your vision, it's important not to overlook two key resources:

- Customers are not only highly qualified, but generally willing to provide input that will help a company figure out what it wants and doesn't want, how it does and doesn't want it delivered, and what elements of the service experience could be changed, improved, or removed for the business to serve them better.
- Front-line employees are armed with an incredible amount of untapped information about customers and the types of service that leave a lasting, *positive* impression on them. And they know from firsthand experience where the weak spots and fail points are in even the most meticulously-designed service delivery systems.

## Words with Meaning

A service vision statement or customer pledge should be able to pass four quick tests:

1. It should be clear, concise, and understandable. Dilbert defines a vision statement as a "long awkward sentence that demonstrates management's inability to think clearly." Make sure you prove the notorious cartoon character wrong.
2. It should communicate, in actionable ways, the things you need to do to satisfy, impress, and keep your customers.
3. It should be consistent with other things you tell employees about the organization's mission and purpose.
4. It should pass the employee "snicker test": Reading it, whether on paper or out loud, should help your people better understand what to do, how to do it, and why to do it, not make them giggle, guffaw, and roll their eyes heavenward. It's important the service vision be ambitious yet grounded in reality—and not written as if it's an advertising slogan.

*Remember:* Knock Your Socks Off Service is mostly a person-to-person activity. If your statement of service focus doesn't make it crystal clear how you want customers to feel (happy, entertained, secure, cared about, like they're dealing with professionals), it isn't complete.

## No Put-On at the Ritz

When you see it done well, you just know it makes sense and helps in everything from measurement to motivation. Consider, for example, Ritz-Carlton Hotels, a two-time winner of the Malcolm Baldrige National Quality Award. The company's service vision was put into words before the first property opened in 1983. Horst Schulze, then president and COO, and his senior managers believed that employees couldn't be expected to deliver first-rate, five-star service if management couldn't define it.

A good part of what Schulze and his management team came up with is embodied in the sixty—three-word statement of the Ritz-Carlton Credo and the twenty "Ritz-Carlton Basics" that define Knock Your Socks Off Service at the Ritz (Figure 10-1).

The service vision is captured by their credo: *"We pledge to provide the finest personal service and facilities for our*

---

### "We Are Ladies and Gentlemen Serving Ladies and Gentlemen."

**The Ritz-Carlton CREDO**

The Ritz-Carlton Hotel is a place where the genuine care and comfort of our guests is our highest mission.

We pledge to provide the finest personal service and facilities for our guests who will always enjoy a warm, relaxed, yet refined ambience.

The Ritz-Carlton experience enlivens the senses, instills well-being, and fulfills even the unexpressed wishes and needs of our guests.

**Three Steps of Service**

1. A warm and sincere greeting. Use the guest name, if and when possible.

2. Anticipation and compliance with guest needs.

3. Fond farewell. Give them a warm good-bye and use their names, if and when possible.

---

### The Ritz-Carlton Basics

1. The Credo will be known, owned and energized by all employees.

2. We are serving "Ladies and Gentlemen serving Ladies and Gentlemen."

3. The three steps of service shall be practiced by all employees.

4. "Smile" – "we are on stage." Always maintain positive eye contact.

5. Use the proper vocabulary with our guests. (Eliminate – Hello, Hi, Ok, Folks)

6. Uncompromising levels of cleanliness are the responsibility of every employee.

7. Create a positive work environment. Practice teamwork and "lateral service."

8. Be an ambassador of your hotel in and outside of the work place. Always talk positively – No negative comments.

9. Any employee who receives a guest complaint "owns" the complaint.

10. Instant guest pacification will be ensured by all. Respond to guest wishes within ten minutes of the request. Follow-up with a telephone call within twenty minutes to ensure their satisfaction.

11. Use guest incident action forms to communicate guest problems to fellow employees and managers. This will help ensure that our guests are never forgotten.

12. Escort guests, rather than pointing out directions to another area of the hotel

13. Be knowledgeable of hotel information (hours of operation, etc.) to answer guest inquiries.

14. Use proper telephone etiquette. Answer within three rings and, with a "smile", ask permission to put a caller on hold. Do not screen calls. Eliminate call transfers when possible.

15. Always recommend the hotel's food and beverage outlets prior to outside facilities.

16. Uniforms are to be immaculate; wear proper footwear (clean and polished) and your correct nametag.

17. Ensure all employees know their roles during emergency situations and are aware of procedures. (Practice fire and safety procedures monthly.)

18. Notify your supervisor immediately of hazards, injuries, equipment or assistance needs you have.

19. Practice energy conservation and proper maintenance and repair of hotel property and equipment.

20. Protecting the assets of a Ritz-Carlton Hotel is the responsibility of every employee.

**Figure 10-1.** Ritz Carlton Creedo.

*guests who will always enjoy a warm, relaxed yet refined am-
biance. The Ritz- Carlton experience enlivens the senses, instills well-being and fulfills even the unexpressed wishes and
needs of our guests."*

The hotel also found it useful to craft a sound bite—"We
are ladies and gentlemen serving ladies and gentlemen"—to
help employees remember the experience they consistently
want to create for guests.

Notice how the Ritz-Carlton service standards—the 20
Basics—are aligned with the credo. For example, the vision
describes creating a "warm, relaxed yet refined ambiance"
which is made actionable for employees with the service standard, "use proper vocabulary with our guests." At the Ritz-
Carlton, casual language like "OK" and "no problem" is replaced with a more refined vernacular like "my pleasure" or
"certainly" to match the environment. The idea isn't to come
off as stuffy or aristocratic, but rather to match the luxurious
and professional setting. As Horst Schulze was fond of saying,
"Elegance without warmth is arrogance."

## Transforming Words to Action

Three steps are integral to formulating the service vision:

1. *Identify your key customers.* For Courtyard by Marriott
Hotels, it's the business traveler, a group that accounts for
most of the hotel's business. That doesn't mean Courtyard
won't jump to serve other customer groups. It just means the
hotel's service vision—"we make it our business to know business travelers"—and delivery systems are designed and managed in a way that ensures the key customer group receives the
customized care and amenities (high speed Internet access,
ample work space in rooms, big continental breakfast to start
the day) to keep it happy and returning again and again.

2. *Identify your core contribution to customers.* For airlines, it's moving things from point A to point B, on time,
safely, with luggage intact and ideally on the same plane as the
passenger who brought it to the airport. For a printing com-

pany, it's meeting the customer's need for high-quality documents that are produced on time and within budgets. In essence, your core contributions are the things you absolutely have to perform well to stay in the business you're in.

3. *Decide what you want to be famous for.* A service vision ought to have some "jump start" component that makes you distinctive and exciting in the eyes of customers. Nordstrom's is well-known for its return policy, Amazon.com and Netflix for how they personalize the buying experience for repeat customers, and outdoor gear store REI for its interactive, "try before you buy" sales approach and customer education. Typically this is where there can be a clear and distinguishable difference between you and your competition. If your customers are going to be out there telling stories about you (the fabled "word of mouth" advertising that consistently proves to be the most persuasive marketing edge you can have), this is what they're going to be talking about.

Once you've formulated your service vision, you must communicate it over and over again. Just as 20:20 vision doesn't help the person who won't watch where he or she is going, your service strategy will mean nothing unless you and your employees can articulate, translate, and act on it.

I wish every employee could read our mission statement and know how it came about.

—Comment from a Frustrated Bank Teller
Penciled on a Service Quality Survey

# 11

# A Service Vision Statement Sampler

Write the vision, and make it plain upon tablets, that all
may readeth it.

—Habakkuk
Old Testament Prophet

To help you craft your own service vision statement, we offer
several examples. Notice that they come in all lengths, styles,
shapes, and sizes. Yours may resemble several, one, or none of
them. What matters is that your statement fits your business
strategy, culture, and your customers.

## Short and Sweet

If brevity is the soul of wit, it's worth measuring the words you
use carefully, making them count, not mount up. Here's how
a convention and exposition management company, a restaurant chain, and an award-winning hospital "cut to the chase."

### The Freeman Companies

The Freeman Companies of Dallas, Texas, is a leading
provider of exposition and convention services, providing
everything from booths, chairs, and displays to labor, electri-

cal power, and shipping services for thousands of trade shows each year.

How Freeman's service quality is rated by customers (trade show exhibitors) depends in large part on if ordered merchandise arrives at their exhibition booths on time and without damage. With an untold number of moving parts involved, managing an exhibition hall requires the precision of a Swiss watch and the timing of a crackerjack pit crew.

Freeman's service vision, highlighted below, was crafted after the company conducted extensive research to determine the key drivers of customer loyalty—those performance factors that make or break a customer's desire to keep doing business with the organization.

*Freeman's service vision statement:* "To support exhibitors, show managers and event professionals in the successful marketing of their products and services by providing highly personalized, proactive solutions delivered by a valued relationship with trusted, accessible experts."

## Country Kitchen

Country Kitchen is a chain of full-service family restaurants that creates loyal customers by continuing to abide by founder Bill Johnson's simple but effective philosophy: "Treat folks special." That service ethic, along with a variety of appetizing food, helped Country Kitchen thrive over the years even as it morphed from a nickel hamburger stand to a breakfast and coffee shop to today's full-service restaurant.

*Country Kitchen's service vision:* "Country Kitchen is where our guests feel like they're coming home, the food is always fresh, the smiles stretch a country mile and breakfast can be anytime of the day."

## Aurora St. Luke's Medical Center

Aurora St. Luke's Medical Center in Milwaukee, Wisconsin has long been recognized for its service quality, innovative health care practices, application of new technologies, and record for patient safety.

*Aurora St. Luke's service vision:* "We are committed to setting the standards of excellence in our profession and our markets. Our innovative technology and progressive attitude attract patients, staff and physicians. Our personalized care and service ensure they return and recommend us to others."

Sometimes articulating the whats, whys, and wherefores of your service strategy seems almost painfully simple—only after, of course, you've completed the often arduous process of crafting it.

As short and simple as many of the best service vision statements are, many companies abbreviate them even further as a means of helping embed them in employees' minds. Walk through Dell Computer's headquarters in Round Rock, Texas, for example, and it's hard to miss one phrase adorning conference rooms and hallways: "The Customer Experience: Own It." Consider creating your own service vision "sound bite" to help guide and inform employees' everyday actions with customers.[1]

## For Public and Private Consumption

A bit more in-depth are the following two examples. Giant Eagle Supermarkets, one of the nation's largest food retailers and distributors, is known for its high-quality produce, meat, and seafood as well as offering a breadth of on-site services including dry cleaning, supervised child learning and activity centers, fuel stations, film laboratories, video rental, and more. Travelocity is one of the leading providers of consumer travel services for leisure and business travels, and is known for providing one-stop internet travel shopping while still providing some of the lowest fares and rates available.

### Giant Eagle

At Giant Eagle, we are committed to helping our customers "Make every day taste better."

---

[1]Karl Albrecht and Ron Zemke, *Service America!* (New York: McGraw-Hill Publications, 2002), p. 108.

We will do so by delivering on our six promises to our customer.

## Our Six Promises to Our Customer

1. We promise to go the extra mile to meet our customers' needs; that we will think like a customer and treat each and every customer based on the Golden Rule.
2. We promise to build and maintain superior stores where we can create an unparalleled shopping experience that is easy, fun, and exciting.
3. We promise that every area of our store will be benchmarked against the best in class, and to bring only the highest quality, widest variety, and most unique array of products and services to our customers.
4. We promise to share our customers' passion for food, and to be a trusted partner in bringing them the best food and food expertise.
5. We promise to give our customers great value for their money.
6. We promise to be a vibrant and active partner in our communities by giving generously of our time, talents, and money at the corporate, store, and individual level.

By delivering on each and every one of these promises, each and every day, Giant Eagle will stand apart from our competition and hold a unique and distinctive place in the minds of our customers.

## Travelocity's Customer "Bill of Rights"

1. *You have the right to get what you booked.* Neither overbooked hotel, nor pool renovation, nor missing rental car, nor lost reservation should stand in the way of you and a smooth trip. That's why Travelocity Guarantees that everything about your booking will be right, or we'll work with our partners to make it right, right away. And that's why this guarantee means that we look out for you from the very moment you book with Travelocity.

2. *You have the right to the best overall value in travel.* Travel enriches your life when it's done right. We understand that on top of a guaranteed low price, travelers need useful, insider information, the security of reliable customer support, and control over the details that make a trip smooth, efficient, and truly great.
3. *You have the right to accurate and objective information upfront.* That's why Travelocity was the first to offer objective travel ratings—not inflated ratings to sell you— and independent reviews where travelers share their experiences, both good and bad. It's also why we give you the full price of your rental car, including the taxes and fees that typically surprise a customer, upfront with car TotalPrice$^{SM}$.
4. *You have the right to a straightforward presentation of your options.* We want you to choose the options that best suit you. If a hotel has rooms available, we won't lead you to believe that the hotel is sold out. We also won't subject you to impossible terms and conditions that make an offer hollow.
5. *You have the right to find what you're looking for quickly and easily.* That's why we redesigned our site for complete ease-of-use so you can find that great last minute deal to Paris, or the best brunch in Salt Lake City (served in a seventy-five-year-old trolley car diner tucked in the hills of Emigration Canyon).
6. *You have the right to speak with someone and get help anytime.* Call one of our knowledgeable representatives for help anytime at 888-872-8356 or 210-521-5871 (for international callers). We're here to help you 24/7.
7. *You have the right to be inspired by your travel company.* Like a well-traveled friend just back from a wine tour of Tuscany, we want to inspire you to see the world.

These are your rights. Take advantage of them. Let nothing stand between you and them—expect maybe a pair of nice sunglasses.

Where there is no vision, the people perish.

—Ecclesiastes

# 12

# Standards and Norms: Delivering on the Service Promise

In essence, if we want to direct our lives, we must take control of our consistent actions. It's not what we do once in a while that shapes our lives, but what we do consistently.

—Anthony Robbins
Motivational Guru

While a service vision describes the experience you want to *create* for customers, a service standard communicates what you strive to *be*—every time, in similar fashion—across the organization so customers can count on a consistent style, attitude, or manner from your staff. A service norm, on the other hand, describes what you strive to *do*, every time, in the same fashion so customers receive consistent action, effort, or execution.

For example, if the service *standard* is "we provide our customers access that is easy and quick, and ensure rapid response to questions or problems" (what employees strive to be), a service *norm* might read, "all associates will be reachable by phone during business hours unless in flight or directly engaged with a customer; all phone calls from customers are returned within the hour, and all e-mails answered with four hours of receipt (what you strive to do).

Why bother creating service standards and norms? For one, they help translate a service vision into concrete goals that your people can easily understand and work toward every day. Standards and norms are also important tools for aligning the organization so that everyone is "rowing together as one." When specific, measurable, and perceived as ambitious but achievable by service staff, standards become a powerful means of communicating performance expectations.

Standards also help create a consistency of experience that builds all-important customer trust. Whether promising package delivery "absolutely, positively" overnight, guaranteeing credit decisions on home mortgage applications within a week, or response to customer phone calls within two hours, regularly living up to the "service promise" builds credibility and creates a bond with customers that becomes difficult to break.

When people know what to expect each and every time they do business with you—caring, knowledgeable, and competent employees that won't let them walk away unhappy—they are more likely to return again with their funds and friends in tow. However if you're seen as erratic and unpredictable—some days delivering on the service promise, other days treating standards as "nice to" but not "need to" achieve performance goals—it creates a sense of unease and distrust that has a corrosive effect on loyalty.

## Build Standards Around Loyalty Factors

The best service standards strike the right balance between customer expectations and internal capabilities. Set the bar too low and you risk offending customers; set it too high and it can frustrate and demoralize employees who, despite their best efforts, regularly fall short of the mark.

When it comes to responsiveness standards, for example, it's a mistake to think customers won't accept anything less than "right this instant." However, giving yourself too much extra wiggle room can make you look slow and indifferent in relation to more nimble competitors.

Start the standards-building process by surveying customers to find out what separates *exemplary* from *satisfactory* performance in their minds, whether it be how quickly you resolve their problems, order delivery expectations, response time to telephone calls or e-mail, or time on hold.

In the dry-cleaning business, for example, there's a big difference between "I have to have this dry cleaning to wear next week," and "I want to have these winter clothes cleaned before I put them away for the season." Use that information to create standards that work well for you and then try them out on customers. Then get their feedback via formal and informal surveys to find out if that timeliness standard works for them. If it doesn't, you can work together to find an alternative.

You'll also want to determine performance thresholds—service areas where, if performance consistently falls below a certain expectation, customers would strongly consider taking their business elsewhere. When leaving a message with a company's voice response system, for example, most customers would, in an ideal world, prefer to hear back within an hour or two—but depending on the urgency of the request might be fine with a satisfactory response on that same day. But wait until the next day or two to return that call—and do so more than once—and it becomes a significant black mark against your organization, pushing customers ever closer to aligning with a more responsive competitor.

Work first to create standards in areas that your research shows have the biggest influence on customer loyalty. Clients may not care that you guarantee to answer the telephone in two rings instead of three—they'd much rather you ensure that whoever picks up on that third ring is equipped to handle their question or solve their problem on first contact in a friendly and efficient manner.

## A Moving Target

Setting service standards and norms isn't a one-time proposition. Customer expectations are constantly in motion, and the more exposure your clients have to service role models, the more rapidly their expectations change. Regular clients of Federal Express, accustomed to its exemplary delivery performance and ability to track packages by the minute, will expect more of the same when they order from your Web site or catalog. Customers of Travelocity or USAA insurance, used to having their questions answered and problems resolved on first contact (and not pulling out their hair trying to find a human being to talk to), won't look kindly on calling your organization and getting passed from Patti to Paul to Penelope—or trapped in voice-mail hell—before finally getting someone who can help them. Those who frequent Amazon.com or Omahasteaks.com will expect to receive immediate e-mail confirmation of orders they've placed on your e-commerce site, as well as acknowledgement of any other e-contact ("we have received your e-mail . . .") within one hour or less of sending it—and sometimes detailed responses to their questions within that same time frame.

These escalated expectations may not mean you have to equal the performance of service exemplars, but it does mean you'll have to elevate your performance to stay competitive and keep these newly enlightened customers coming back for more.

In e-commerce, for example, responsiveness has emerged as a growing driver of customer loyalty, and plenty of Web sites continue to fall short of customer expectations in that area. A study from Jupiter Research, an international research organization, found that only 45 percent of Web sites resolve e-mail inquires from customers within twenty-four hours, and some 39 percent took three days or longer to reply to e-mail—or didn't respond at all. The number of such sites has grown 7 percent year over year from 2000 to 2005, according to the study. "This growing segment of unresponsive companies is damaging customer loyalty and retention," says Zachary McGeary, a Jupiter associate analyst and author of the research report.[1]

---

[1]"U.S. Customer Service and Support Metrics" a study conducted by Jupiter Research, December 2005.

The bottom line is to make sure your standards for response time to customer e-mail are pegged to "Internet time," not the rhythms of your own internal company systems. It's a message organizations would do well to remember when creating standards for any facet of their customer service performance.

## Standards and Norms in Action

Banco Popular North America, a Chicago, Illinois-based bank with branches in six states, has developed a reputation for impressive service quality and progressive people practices that have led to honors like being named one of *Fortune* magazine's "100 Best Companies To Work For" in 2005.

We've included a selection of the bank's service standards and norms, along with its service vision, to illustrate how those three elements—when well-constructed and aligned— lay the foundation for creating Knock Your Socks Off service. Banco Popular, like other customer-centric organizations, understands that unless standards and norms are clearly written, specific, and measurable—and employees are consistently held accountable for achieving them—they are little more than empty promises or slogans hanging on the wall.

### Banco Popular's Service Vision

"We are here for one purpose: to deliver consistently engaging and caring experiences for our customers. Their needs and dreams drive us, their challenges unite us, and our values guide us in delivering trusted financial solutions. Our dream makers' (what the bank calls its employees) pride and passion are contagious."

### Standards and Norms

*People Standard:* Dream makers are dedicated, resourceful, and caring people who share and demonstrate our values and commitment for the customer and each other.

*Norm:* Our people are:

- Team oriented and believe in our mission and embrace our diversity and heritage.
- Look for ways to add value to the customer *and* the bank.
- Use sound judgment in making decisions on behalf of the customer *and* the bank.

*Communications Standard:* Our communication is timely, clear, and consistent.
  *Norm:* We:

- Never use e-mail or voicemail when we need to have a personal conversation.
- Communicate clearly about deliverables to manage expectations.
- Help our people "connect the dots" by including the "why" in communications.

*Responsiveness Standard:* We respond with a sense of urgency to our customers and coworkers.
  *Norm:* We:

- Respond to customer calls within one hour; internal telephone calls or e-mails within the same day.
- Provide solutions or updates the next business day.
- When out of the workplace on business, we check daily for customer calls or e-mails and respond or delegate accordingly on the same day.

*Accuracy Standard:* We do it right the first time, every time.
  *Norm:* We:

- Treat every transaction as if it were our own or that of a beloved family member.
- Clarify and confirm requests to ensure we understand the need and execute with precision.
- Are thorough and complete in everything we do.

*Accountability Standard:* Each of us is accountable to ensure every interaction with a customer or coworker is managed in a positive and purposeful way.

*Norms:* We:

- Treat every customer as if Robert (the bank's president) sent them to us.
- Own and stay connected to the customer's request from beginning to end and then follow-up, being accountable for the outcome. We are "links in a chain" working together for the benefit of the customer.
- Act in the best interest of the customer and build trust by personally facilitating any necessary hand-off (to a coworker).

## Consistency Breeds Trust

Service standards and norms are a pledge to customers that you'll be the same reliable and responsive organization each time they do business with you, not blow hot or cold depending on management's fickle agenda—"last month we focused on service, this month we're back to productivity"—or the state of the last quarterly financial report. Tying standards to performance factors that have the biggest impact on customer loyalty, then being vigilant in measuring, adjusting, and delivering on them to ensure you meet customers' shifting expectations, is one of the surest ways to build customer trust and create distinction in your industry.

Consistency is the foundation of virtue.

—Sir Francis Bacon
English Statesman and Philosopher

# Imperative 4

# Make Your Service Delivery System ETDBW (Easy To Do Business With)

Your service delivery system is all of the apparatus, physical and procedural, that the employees of your organization must have at their disposal to meet customers' needs and to keep the service promises you make to your customers. A well-designed service delivery system will make you easy to do business with. What your service strategy promises is what your system must deliver. Every time.

If your promise is, "twenty-four-hour delivery on all orders—no exceptions," your service delivery system is everything you do and use to make twenty-four-hour delivery a reality, from your order entry system to the way you measure your performance.

In a badly designed and poorly operating delivery system, you frequently hear *managers* complaining about lazy, unmotivated employees, *front-line employees* complaining about stupid, unreasonable customers, and *customers* complaining about inflexible, unhelpful people and rules. A well-done service delivery system is customer- and employee-friendly and has monitors and feedback mechanisms to enable the people who work in the system to correct poor results.

Your continuing quest should be to seek out ways of making it easier for your customers to do business with you tomorrow than it was for them to do business with you last year, last month, last week, and last night.

Rest assured, that's exactly what your competition is doing.

# 13

# Bad Systems Undermine Good People

You can take great people, highly trained and motivated, and put them in a lousy system and the system will win every time.

—Geary Rummler
Founding Partner
Performance Design Lab

A friend/colleague of ours tells the story of going to the grocery store one evening to buy food for the family of a friend who was spending a few days in the hospital. When she asked about getting a deli tray, she was informed by the night clerk that the woman who made them up had already left for the evening. "I didn't know making deli trays was such a specialized skill," was her first response. But meats and cheeses still seemed like a good idea, so she decided to create her own deli assortment piece by piece.

She asked the clerk to thin-slice a half pound of ham. He did, wrapping the slices in waxed butcher paper, writing the price on the package and putting it on the deli counter. The process was repeated with turkey, then roast beef, then Swiss cheese, then . . . About the time our friend had more than $20 worth of food on the counter, she noticed a stack of large empty plastic deli trays on a back table. Sudden inspiration: "How much for one of those with a plastic lid?"

"Lady," came the tart response, "you can't buy a tray unless you buy a *tray*."

"Excuse me?"

"YOU CAN'T GET A TRAY UNLESS YOU GET A *TRAY*."

Her first thought was that she was dealing with a frontline person in desperate need of a personality transplant. Belatedly, she realized the real issue: the store's inventory control *system* was based on counting the trays. It wasn't that the clerk didn't want to help her. He just couldn't see how to.

The system won. The customer lost. The front-line person lost, too. The people who decided to use deli trays as a financial control device no doubt had the best of intentions. But they were blind to the effects of their decision on customers. And the organization's obviously well-communicated insistence on following procedures to the letter stopped the front-line service person in his tracks.

Yes, you need systems. But rules, policies, and procedures should be servants, not masters. In a world where most services are readily available from multiple sources, it is important to make the system component of the service transaction at a minimum painless and easy, at best invisible or positively memorable.

Your front-line people have nothing but the system and their own skills to use in satisfying customers. A well-designed service system must have two attributes if it is to help them do that consistently:

1. *Service delivery systems should be "easy on the front line."* Service delivery systems are not a naturally occurring phenomenon in nature. People make them up. People should be able to explain them, adjust them, and change them—and even circumvent them on those occasions when a customer comes in from an angle no system designer could ever have foreseen. The people with the power to flex the systems should be the ones at the front line.

2. *Service delivery systems should be "easy* for *the front line."* If the rules, policies, and procedures get in the way of giving great service, your people will in time stop focusing on their roles and start focusing on their restrictions. As one veteran of the front-line wars told us, "If I'm on the front line and customers bitch about barriers I can't better or bypass, I'll become a bastard or burn out."

## The Human Factor

There's a very real people dimension to the system dilemma. It's usually expressed in the lament, "You just can't get good people anymore." Wrong. We would argue that generations of experience with dysfunctional and sometimes downright abusive service systems have taught our front-line people—and our customers—a lot of bad habits, attitudes, and behaviors. The people at the front line have learned to duck and cover because what hits the fan hits them from every direction.

For years, higher-ups have preached conformity to rules and regulations, policies and procedures, accountability and control—and made a point of punishing people who got a little uppity and tried to do more than they were allowed to do. As a result, customers faced with inflexible people—and their inflexible rules—learned to get nasty if they wanted to receive anything beyond what company policy mandated. It's truly a vicious circle.

If you think your staff has more than its share of poor service performers, try fixing the system to make it more livable and responsive for everyone involved. You'll be amazed by the human changes you'll create.

## The Law of Rules

Your task as a manager is to set up workflows, guidelines, procedures, and fail-safes that your people can readily customize or tweak to meet the specific needs and expectations of your customers. It's inevitable that rules will be written or evolve over time. The "good rules" will serve your people—and through them your customers—well. The "bad rules" will seek to enslave. How do you know which is which?

- Good rules *are grounded in customer expectations and contribute to meeting customer needs.* Making answering the phone by the third ring into a rule won't help the customer whose call is answered in staccato fashion and put on hold before a word can be inserted edgewise because your people are working only to hit the statistical target.
- Good rules *help the customer experience the service provider as "easy to do business with."* Put yourself in your customer's shoes: Do the steps you're asked to take make sense or make extra work for you?
- Good rules *are consistent with the partnership (co-creator) dimension of service.* If your customers are truly your partners, then the pieces and parts of your service system have to provide mutual benefits. They need to help you serve *and* they need to help your customers/partners tell you how you can serve them better.
- Good rules *have feedback woven in.* They have a system monitoring component that alerts your people in a prompt and actionable fashion whenever the delivery system is about to fail or break. That way you can fix it before your customer experiences the disappointment of service breakdown.
- Good rules *allow your front-line people to be human, not robots.* They allow—even encourage—your people to respond uniquely, personally, and creatively to the full spectrum of customer needs and expectations and especially to those that do not fit the standard pattern.
- Good rules *remind everyone that they are guidelines to promote a value or goal, not the value or goal itself.* Like our rule-restricted deli clerk, if your people follow the letter of the law but miss the value or goal, they've failed themselves, the organization, and most especially the customer.

When applied without customer focus to a service delivery system, the production mind-set (with its focus on control, uniformity, scientific method, and linear thinking) leads to noncreative, nonresponsive people and actions. It causes service people to "step over dollars to pick up dimes." And all in full view of the customer—who's usually expecting much better of you.

In designing and continuously evaluating your fail-safe service system, remember that it's the *customer's* need that is driving the game. As Harvard marketing professor Theodore Levitt once put it, the customer would like to go from "I need a quarter-inch hole" to "I have a quarter-inch hole" without having to deal with quarter-inch drill bits and hardware stores and chucks and electric cords and checkout counters. The smart service provider designs and maintains the delivery system accordingly.

Service systems that are low on the friendliness scale tend, by their very design, to subordinate convenience and ease of access for the customer in favor of the convenience of the people within the system.

—Karl Albrecht
Coauthor, *Service America
in the New Economy*

# 14

# Fix the System, Not the People

Eighty percent of customers' problems are caused by
bad systems, not by bad people.

—John Goodman
Vice Chairman of TARP, Inc.

Your people can only be as good as your system allows them
to be. So ask yourself how much of the complexity and hassle
you can siphon out of your system. The simpler, faster, and
easier you can make it for your customers—and your employees—the more willing and skilled they'll become at making
use of it.

America Online found out just how much damage a
poorly designed service system can do to a reputation for customer service in summer 2006. The problem began when AOL
customer Vincent Ferrari of the Bronx, New York, called the
company with a simple request to cancel his membership. But
rather than encountering a quick, hassle-free transaction,
Ferrari found himself in a "wild, horrifying descent into customer service hell," according to *The New York Times*.

Simply put, AOL sought to make it as difficult as possible
for Ferrari to end his relationship with the company. The AOL
customer service representative who took his call refused
to comply when, over and over again, Ferrari asked to close
his account. During the conversation Ferrari used the word

"cancel" more than twenty-one times, all for naught as the single-minded service rep worked doggedly to find a way to keep him on board.

We know all of this because the customer recorded five minutes of the conversation and then posted the audio file on his blog, which got so many visitors when word spread—300,000 in one day—that it crashed his server. Because of that exposure, Ferrari appeared on NBC's "Today" show and his encounter was replayed on numerous national radio shows.

Was this simply the case of a rogue customer service rep overstepping his boundaries? The audio recording indicates otherwise—that he was likely following company policy. As the *Times* reported, "Had John (the self-identified service rep) been in the grip of genuine pathological madness, the recording of the call wouldn't have drawn the attention of so many people. What one hears in John is an actor performing clumsily, to be sure, but someone working from a script provided by his employer that confuses 'customer service' with 'sales.'"

Devising strategies to retain customers who are thinking about leaving you is smart business; working to save existing customers who are "at risk" is almost always less costly than trying to recruit new ones. Yet when front-line employees aren't taught when to call off the dogs—when policies explicitly or implicitly encourage them to turn a deaf ear to customers who are resolute in a desire to cancel accounts or make other transactions—service systems and policies become the antithesis of "easy to do business with." And as AOL so painfully discovered, the advent of blogs and online discussion boards means that customers victimized by such policies will often send word of their shabby treatment spreading across the planet like wildfire.

## Warning Signs

Any time you hear a sales or service person—or yes, even a manager—say things like the following to a customer, you are listening to a service delivery system that is not easy to do business with:

- "I'm sorry, it's against policy."
- "Well, just wait a couple more days. I'm sure the package will show up soon."
  *Customer:* "Can I ask you a question?"
  *Service Rep:* "Could you make it quick, I've got a meeting to go to."
- "Ma'am, we wouldn't have given your name to a collection agency if you hadn't been billed at *least* twice for the overdue payment."
- "Oh, that's a sales floor (or warehouse or accounting or field service) problem. I'm in customer service. No, I don't have that number."
- "My computer is down, can you call back later?"
- "Your call is very important to us. Your wait time is approximately 30 minutes."
- "I know you're not ready to leave yet, but would you mind paying your bill? I'm going off duty in fifteen minutes."

And the all-time battle cry of the dysfunctional service system:

- "You have to understand how we do business around here."

## Developing Easy To Do Business With Thinking

The operative theme is being "easy to do business with" (ETDBW). It's important to note that *easy* means "comfortable" but not always "simple." Sometimes service delivery systems are necessarily complex, requiring that customers go through multiple steps or interact with employees from different departments to get questions answered or needs met. What's essential is that any system, regardless if it contains a mountain or a molehill of Moments of Truth, be designed in a way that ensures customers experience a minimum of hassle, dissonance, or anxiety. That to us signals *easy*. Every dollar and every hour you spend anticipating and removing barriers to customer access, comfort, and support will come back to you tenfold.

Dell Computer exhibited ETDBW thinking, for example, when it announced that it planned to gradually reduce the number of product rebates it offers to customers, opting instead to lower the baseline price of its personal computers. Why make that change, especially considering the important role that rebates play in advertising the company's low prices? Dell's research found that customers simply didn't like the hassle of dealing with rebate procedures.

Several hotels had ETDBW in mind when they devised more hassle-free guest check-in procedures. Rather than making travel-weary guests wait in line or deal with paperwork at the front desk, they installed self-service check-in kiosks in their lobbies. Slide a credit card through the kiosk and—voilà—your room keys emerge. Hilton and Hyatt Hotels also have been allowing some members of their loyalty programs to check in remotely via the Web, and Ritz-Carlton Hotels allow guests staying on the club level to bypass hotel lobby registration and check in directly on the club level floor. The hotels say these new check-in options are designed for those who prefer speed and efficiency over the personal touch provided by front desk staff.[1]

ETDBW service systems are designed through the eye of the customer, not through the lens of internal staff. As Karl Albrecht and Ron Zemke explain in their book *Service America in the New Economy*, (McGraw-Hill, 2002), "when you allow an organizational system to evolve on its own, you can be fairly sure it will evolve in the direction of self-convenience, becoming introverted rather than outward-focused. Introversion results in complicated procedures that customers don't understand, bureaucracy that drains resources, and policies that pass customers off from department to department, rather than answering their questions or solving their problems on first contact."

[1]"Tough Market Drives Changes at Intel," Dell, Gateway," *USA Today*, July 14, 2006.

While ETDWB characteristics are vital for success in any business environment, they take on even more importance in the online world. For example, a mediocre restaurant known for an indifferent wait staff that sits in the heart of a major business district will continue to do good business just by virtue of its prime location. On the Web there is no such proximity; you can't depend on customers to just "wander by" or visit your e-commerce site because it's so convenient. That places a premium on service factors like user-friendly site design, providing one-click access to any page on the site, ensuring a painless check-out process, allowing easy price searches, and giving customers ample ways to find help, including an 800 number, when they have questions.

One of the chief ways companies become "difficult to do business with" is by making it next to impossible to find a human being to talk to. Paul English, an entrepreneur and technology expert, grew so frustrated with the challenge of trying to track down carbon-based life forms in organizations' voice response systems that he developed and published a "cheat sheet" on his blog naming companies and the codes needed to reach an operator—codes not made public by the companies. Needless to say, his list became an online phenomenon and English a hero of frustrated consumers everywhere.

Most organizations will say they avoid making it easy to find live help because phone calls represent the most costly and labor intensive of all contact channels. Yet research from the Center for Client Retention in Springfield, New Jersey, an organization that surveys customers who use call centers, suggests how short-sighted that view can be. Customers who interact with human beings on the phone are more likely than other clients to "volunteer useful information, try out a new product and come away with a strong sense of loyalty" to the organization.

Failure to provide easy access to live help can have particularly devastating consequences for customer loyalty when people encounter problems. A 2006 study by Customer Care Measurement and Consulting (CCMC), a leading customer research and consulting firm based in Alexandria, Virginia, found that being forced to use automated telephone technology without an option to talk to a live service agent had a highly negative impact on complainants' satisfaction levels. Not providing an "opt out" to live help scored 83rd out of 85 customer care practices the CCMC asked survey respondents to rate for service-friendliness in a national study of corporate customer complaint-handling processes.[2]

## Easy To Do Business With Quick Test

How good are you right now? How many times do you have to wonder "Where did the system break down" and "Where did the customer get lost" and "How can we rewrite the rules, change the policies, or upgrade the gear to keep this from happening again?" The more you ask (and answer) those questions in the short term, the less you'll face them as problems in the long term.

Here's a little ETDBW experiment to find out where you are right now.

1. Go out for lunch or coffee, or do something to get you out of the building.
2. Call home—back to your office/department/store, using the general, in-the-phonebook number, not the one you know to call when you want fast action.
3. Without identifying yourself (disguise your voice if you have to), ask for something you know to be difficult or strange, but doable, from the person who answers the telephone.
4. Count the following:
   Number of times you are put on hold.
   Number of times you are transferred.
   Number of people who say, "Gee, I'm not sure we do that . . ." or some variation.

[2]Marc Grainer, Jeff Maszal, and Scott Broetzmann, "Why the Customer Care Revolution Has Failed: How Companies Misuse the Telephone When Responding to Customers," *CCMC*, April 2006.

ETDBW Scores

| | |
|---|---|
| 125-150: | Genius—Your systems are an asset. |
| 100-124: | Average—Your systems aren't any worse than anybody else's. |
| 75-99: | Slow—Your systems are a detriment to customer retention. |
| below 75: | Disabled—Your systems are probably driving customers away in droves. Immediate remedial action indicated. |

Number of people who explain why they can't honor your request because "it's not how we do business here," talk about why their day is going so badly or why your request is such a bother.

Number of people who tell you, "No, you can't have that," in some form or another.

Number of times you have to ask to speak to someone else or someone in charge.

Number of times you have to repeat yourself.

Multiply the result by 10 and subtract from 150 to arrive at your "Easy To Do Business With" quotient. Your ETDBW quotient is like an IQ: The lower it is, the harder you are to do business with.

## Improving Your Easy To Do Business With IQ

So what does an ETDBW service delivery system look like in action? From the customer's point of view, the "customer friendliest" delivery systems are:

1. *Accessible.* You can reach the company easily and when you want to—including finding live phone help.
2. *Accurate.* Whether it's about shipments, billing, or status, the information is accurate and correct.

3. *Integrated.* Customers can get all the information they need from one point of contact—ideally the first.

4. *Customer-Driven.* Customers can understand and use the information they're given without hiring an interpreter, having to repeatedly call your 800 number or needing to refer to a pile of order and billing code numbers.

5. *Fast.* Customers never have the sense they are waiting for a very slow computer to get warmed up or that their order is making the trip from Phoenix to Boston via rickshaw or pedicab. When customers call your 800 line, they aren't placed on hold so long that they can cook a turkey, finish the Sunday *Times* crossword and realphabetize their DVD collection before your service reps answer.

6. *Easy to Understand.* In our current era of outsourcing and global service, customers are often served by pleasant, competent people in faraway lands who seemed to have learned to speak the customer's language using a correspondence course. Customers don't mind if the service rep is in Bombay or Singapore; they *do* mind if they have to work hard to understand the server or be understood by the server.

7. *Totally Transparent.* If there are hoops to be jumped through or marathons to be run, they happen outside of the customer's field of vision.

## How to Change a "Not so Easy To Do Business With" System

- *Do not* go out and start buying new computers or servers, upgraded customer relationship management (CRM) software or a new phone system.
- *Do not* go out and hire a pack of expensive management consultants.
- *Do not* blame, punish, or execute your front-line people.
- *Do* get as much up-to-date customer input as possible. What specifically are customers complaining about?

- *Do* spend time observing what customers are experiencing. Put yourself in the customer's shoes and work to see the system from their point of view.
- Talk with people who are likely to know what customers *really* fuss about. One hotel manager held frequent focus groups with the taxi drivers that took guests from the hotel to the airport. The guest who might have replied "fine" to the front desk clerk's "How was your stay?" query might give a different evaluation to the taxi driver.
- *Do* start with a series of small meetings with customer contact employees and employees who directly support their work. (Don't make the meetings too small or people will be reluctant to tell you what they really think or so large that most people feel like spectators.) In those meetings ask two questions:

  1. What do our customers like least about doing business with us?
  2. What can we do to make it easier for you to serve the customer?

Then shut up, listen, thank people for their candor and take notes. You won't necessarily like the answers, and they may not all be immediately actionable, but they will give you a great start at making your company, department, or team Easy To Do Business With.

> We believe that our activities should be governed by the needs and desires of our customers rather than by our internal requirement and insights.
>
> —Eugene F. McCabe
> Vice President, Marketing
> Merck Sharpe & Dohme

# 15

# Measure and Manage from the Customer's Point of View

The four most important words in service quality are: measure, measure, measure, and measure.

—Ken Dagley
President, Australian Customer
Service Association

Regardless of the business you are in and the size of your operation, measure you must! A commitment to service quality without a commitment to standards and measurement is a dedication to lip service, not customer service. Standards and measurement are critical to the smooth functioning—and improvement—of your service delivery system. While measurements come in many forms and serve different purposes, all share the same goal—creating a trusted guidance system for managers' decision making.

A common denominator among companies with reputations for high quality service is their bias for setting service standards and their prodigious efforts to measure how well

107

those standards are met. In complex service delivery systems—like those of United Parcel Service, Enterprise Rent-
a-Car or Southwest Airlines—that effort involves hundreds
of standards and a multitude of measurement systems to
keep service delivery on an even keel. In a simpler system,
like that of a Chick-fil-A restaurant or the FedEx Kinko's
Copies down on the corner, it takes far fewer standards
and measures to keep on top of the "How are we doing?"
question.

## The Look of Customer-Focused Measurement

Chances are pretty good that your company already measures
a number of things about the service delivery systems you
manage all or part of. Just the same, it is a good idea to stop,
step back from your system for a moment, and ask yourself
whether your current measurement is driven by customer parameters or internal technical specs. To make sure the former,
not the latter, energizes your measurement efforts, use these
three general criteria for auditing—and perhaps improving—
the customer focus of your service delivery system.

1. *Your measurements should reflect your "purpose."*
Nothing makes your service vision—your purpose—more real
to your front-line employees than measuring what you're doing against customer-focused norms.

If your service promise is for "timely deliveries on all
shipments" and your customers have told you that means "24-
hour turnaround on all orders," measure that. But don't just
look inside. You're not done until the customer has taken delivery, so be sure you also measure the customer's perception
of whether or not orders are arriving "in a timely fashion."
Even if you're dead solid certain that a customer's order came
and went in twenty-four hours—and twenty-four hours is
twice as good as your nearest competitor—if the customer
doesn't "feel" that the order arrived in a timely fashion, the
customer is right and you are wrong.

*Remember:* For the customer, *perception* is all there is!

How can you be 100 percent "on time" but wrong about being "timely"?

First, the twenty-four-hour standard is *your* technical standard, not the customer's. To the customer, "timely" is a perception, not a measurement, as it is to you.

Second, "timely" or "on-time" to you typically means when the order goes out *your* door. To customers, those same words may well mean the time the order comes in *their* door, is on the shelf in *their* warehouse, or is in hand and ready for distribution or use in *their* system.

Not your problem? *Wrong!* If your customers believe there is a problem, there is a problem—whether you think it's real or not. And you'd better have a systematic way of finding out about it. Your measurement system has to tell you about the problems customers are perceiving, and as soon as possible, not just comfort you with statistics about your adherence to your own technical standards.

2. *Your measurements should measure customer quality, not just technical quality.* There is a vital difference between the two.

*Technical quality* is the measurement of all the mechanical and procedural things that must go right if your system is to work effectively and efficiently. Technical quality measures are *internal* indicators of your delivery system's specification driven performance.

*Think:* Down time, order waiting time, order assembly time, back order volume, order turnaround time, shipments per hour, time per phone call, and similar measures.

*Customer quality* is the performance of your service delivery system from the *customer's* point of view. It is the assembly of elements that are important to the customer, as judged by the customer. These are the elements that are directly observable by the customer and that most directly determine their satisfaction with your service delivery system.

*Think:* Ease of contact, order correctness and completeness, timeliness of order arrival, courtesy and empathy

of people dealt with, look of package upon arrival, un-
derstandability of the bill, and similar subjective im-
pressions.

Technical quality measures are important to trouble spotting,
problem solving, and the smooth and cost-effective functioning of the system. Customer quality measures are important to
customer delight and retention and to system improvement
and priority setting.

## Measuring What Matters to Customers

Whether they're designed to gauge quantitative or qualitative
service dimensions, your customer-focused measures are
meaningless if they measure the wrong things. Make sure your
survey questions assess the service factors that customers believe are essential to winning their loyalty, not performance
areas that market researchers or line managers assume are critical to keeping them coming back for more.

In organizations with extensive telephone customer contact, for example, the two most common measurements of the
delivery system are length of telephone calls and number of
rings before pickup. Yet customers we've asked about contact
with such companies seldom if ever mention either factor.
They're more concerned about getting the information they
need, having their problems solved (ideally during that first
contact), and not being put on hold for hours or connected to
the voicemail system from hell.

In some companies, these two measures have been automated and computerized as an employee surveillance and
evaluation system. The claim is that such measurement systems improve service. They do not. They *may* improve productivity, which may or may not be related, but service is *not*
the point of such measurement systems. Authority and accountability are.

Not only do they not have the desired effect on customers,
they also don't do a thing to help the people charged with delivering customer service. We've yet to talk to a front-line ser-

vice worker hooked up to one of these electronic stopwatch systems who didn't: (1) resent the obvious lack of trust and (2) learn to trick the system anyway in self-defense. (How? Easy: Watch the time and hang up in mid-sentence when the call starts to go too long. If and when the mystified—or disgruntled—customer calls back, apologize . . . and blame it on "equipment failure.")

Are we suggesting that you not measure "number of rings before answer" or "length of talk-time with customer"? No. We are saying that these and similar measurements, valuable as they may be for managing costs and monitoring system capacity, are not necessarily helping you manage service quality as perceived by your customer. And that means they're not helping—and may well be hindering—your people as they try to directly improve customer satisfaction and directly build customer retention.

## The Customer Service Dashboard

Think of the array of data available to help guide your staff's customer service performance as a "dashboard" of sorts. When driving a car it's essential to keep your eyes on the road and use your senses to successfully navigate, but doing so while ignoring the fuel or temperature gauge is asking for trouble. Likewise, as a service manager you rely on your eyes and ears to evaluate how your staff is performing, but leaning too heavily on qualitative or subjective measures can provide a skewed vision of service quality.

"That's why it's important to create the right dashboard—the right kind and number of formal metrics—to successfully guide and improve service performance," says John Patterson, president of Atlanta-based Progressive Insights Inc., a consulting firm that specializes in helping organizations effectively manage change built around employee and customer loyalty.

Customer service metrics can take on a life of their own unless they are aligned with an organization's key business strategies, policies, processes, and systems, Patterson says.

For example, when developing a list of metrics to be included on your dashboard, ask the question: Does the organization have clear service standards, policies, and procedures that promote partnership between and among units, not just good teamwork within units? Without any cross-unit service metrics, it's difficult to get early warning on the emergence of "silo" thinking that can prevent the kind of seamless, easy-to-do-business with service delivery that creates loyal customers.

Every service dashboard should include four types of metrics, Patterson says:

1. *Course metrics assess whether the organization is "on course" or is pursuing the direction intended.* Typical customer service course metrics might include quantitative measures like number of customers retained, customers' estimated lifetime value or profit per customer. Qualitative course metrics might be anecdotal comments from customers that suggest progress ("you come highly recommended from a friend") or improvement ("your call center representatives seem more efficient and friendly").

2. *Correction metrics include tools to facilitate progress and maintain service effectiveness.* These are the means by which an organization gains a deeper and more complete understanding of course metrics. Quantitative service correction metrics might include measuring customer retention by particular product line or customer segment, customer satisfaction scores by type of customer, length of customer relationship or "share of wallet" by segment. Qualitative correction metrics are things like types of customer complaints, types of errors that trigger refunds or reasons customers give for leaving. Identifying the right *correction* metric starts with a dissection of the *course* metric. For example, if a key course metric is the number of customers under age 25 who re-enroll in a program after one year, the correction metrics might be derived from interviews with those who stay versus those who leave to find out major reasons for both.

3. *Caution metrics provide intelligence needed to shape or change strategic direction and keep pace with shifting customer needs.* This is data vital to effective early warning.

Quantitative caution metrics might be those associated with long-range demographic variations, industry projections, and anticipated psychographic changes in a target customer population. Qualitative caution metrics could be results from focus groups, pilot tests, and futuring studies.

4. *Context metrics are tools to better understand the marketplace and how your business unit or organization compares relative to that environment.* These metrics paint a picture of the setting in which the organization is operating at a given point in time, and help to ensure you don't become so myopic or inwardly focused that competitive mistakes are made. Quantitative context metrics include how other similar organizations are faring in the same market conditions—data like same store customer churn compared to competitors or industry standing in revenue per employee. Qualitative metrics are things like how often the company is favorably mentioned in trade journal or business magazine articles, rankings in independent surveys, or recognition from your industry or profession.

## The Ultimate Survey Question

The quantity and quality of questions chosen for customer surveys and who you choose to send those surveys to, can make all the difference between generating highly useful, actionable feedback and the kind of data does little to drive meaningful service improvement. In an article in the *Harvard Management Update* titled "The Top 10 Reasons You Don't Understand Your Customers," Fred Reichheld, director emeritus at Bain & Company and an expert on customer retention strategies, argued that companies include too many questions on customer satisfaction surveys, send them to the wrong people (read: not key decision makers), and often fail to ask the "ultimate" question that every formal survey should include.

Loading up surveys with too many questions increases measurement costs, discourages potential respondents, and reduces the sample size, Reichheld claims. "Conventional surveys ask so many questions that they typically draw responses only from the bored, the lonely, and the seriously aggrieved," he says.

Reichheld believes there is one question every satisfaction survey should feature but that too often goes missing: *How likely are you to recommend this company to a friend or relative?* Ask the question regularly, he suggests, and then score results on a zero to ten scale: "You'll find out how many of your customers are loyal promoters (9s and 10s), how many are just passively doing business with you (7s and 8s) and how many are detractors (everyone else). The key to driving improved revenues and profit? Creating more promoters and fewer detractors."

As a supervisor or first-line manager, you may not have a lot of control over what gets measured and how it gets measured. But by thinking about what your current measurement does and does not give you, and how you are and are not using the results, you can affect the performance of your delivery system. And if you're not getting the kind of data you need—or getting too much of the wrong kind of data—it's in your interest to build a case with the keepers of the measurement flame for changing this unproductive state of affairs. And the sooner the better!

'Tain't nowhere near right, but it's approximately correct.

—Howland Owl
(Pogo's Quality Guru, explaining the inbred weaknesses of all measurement systems)

# 16

# Add Magic: Creating the Unpredictable and Unique

He who gives great service gets great returns.
—Elbert Hubbard
Nineteenth Century American Writer

Great systems, well-designed and managed, start with a simple goal: reliability—delivering on your *core promise* to the customer. An airline that promises to take you from New York to Minneapolis, but deposits you in Indianapolis instead, does not make you a happy traveler, no matter how friendly the cabin crew, or how smooth the ride.

But that's just for starters. How do you compete for customers when you are one of three airlines, each boasting five flights a day between New York and Minneapolis, all of which deliver passengers to the right "apolis" safely, on time, and with most of their luggage in hand?

Taking off and landing uneventfully will make you just one of three carriers that meet the basic core requirements of air transportation. To distinguish yourself in highly competitive, "me-too" markets, your systems will need to help you reliably and consistently offer something "extra" that draws business away from your competitors. We call the extra dimension that creates indelible customer memories *service magic.*

## Adding Magic

Service magic, much like stage magic, is not simply serendipity or fluke but a set of learned skills developed from desire and mastered by planning, practice, and a keen understanding of the customer psyche. In a nutshell, service magic is about creating memorable surprises for customers who have come to expect the bland, indifferent customer service that characterizes so many transactions in today's business world.

What service magic *is not* is value-added service as most of us know it. Ask customers what actions they consider value-added and they will focus on taking the expected experience to the next step, "they gave me more than I anticipated." Value added is a predictable linear response: the upgrade, the complimentary dessert, or discount coupon for the next visit. It has its own importance and place in the service experience, as we'll explore later in the chapter. However, service magic is unpredictable and unique. When you are left thinking, "I wouldn't have thought of that" you have probably witnessed service magic. We like to think of it as service with imagination more than service with generosity.

Consider this situation. A customer traded in an older model car for a new one. A week after owning the car, she turned on the radio for the first time to discover the dealership had programmed the radio stations from her old car's radio into the new one. That bit of unexpected personalization created a small thrill of magic for the customer.

There also was magic in the actions of a doorman at the Ritz-Carlton Buckhead in Atlanta when he seized the initiative to create a lasting memory for a guest. The customer had flown in to the hotel and was awaiting the arrival of his wife, who had chosen to drive to the site. He had already checked in and was standing in the lobby chatting with the doorman, passing time until his spouse joined him. Eventually the doorman asked, "You're pretty excited about her coming in, aren't you?" and the traveler said that he was. "May I ask her favorite drink?" the doorman said, and the guest replied with "ice cold Absolut with extra lime." The doorman suggested that they surprise her by getting the cherished drink from the bar, putting it on a silver tray, and serving it to her as soon as she pulled in to the hotel. "You just let me know which car is hers when she pulls up out front," the doorman said.

Later, as she stepped from the car, the doorman approached, offered the drink, addressed her by name and said, "I believe you're looking for this . . . and oh, your husband is waiting for you in the lobby. Have a great weekend."

The power of such thoughtful, beyond-the-norm actions lies in their uniqueness. A steady diet of such extravagance and not only can you abuse the bottom line, you risk turning the unique into the usual . . . and the magic vanishes. The trick is to teach your staff how to pick its spots and seek out the small magical touches that, by virtue of their novelty, have a disproportionately large impact on customer memories.

## Using Preplanned Value-Addeds

While service magic is the gold standard of customer delight, the preplanned value-added is a close runner-up in terms of fostering customer loyalty. Used wisely, such tools are an effective complement to magical interludes.

The frequent-customer programs developed as value-addeds by airlines, hotels, car rental companies, and even department stores and grocery stores, are clearly preplanned. But such orchestrated "extras" don't have to be predictable or bland, as guests of the Hotel Monaco in downtown Chicago will gladly tell you. First-time visitors checking into the hotel usually do a double take when the front desk clerk gives them a room key, offers directions to their room, and offers to provide them special companionship by having a goldfish in a gorgeous glass bowl delivered to their room.

For the confused—and who wouldn't be?—the desk person explains: "We're a pet friendly hotel. Since you don't have a pet with you, we'd be pleased to loan you one of ours." The piscatorial value added has gone over so big that many repeat guests ask for a specific fish—by name.

The goldfish is only the opening salvo in the Hotel Monaco's attempts to impress with preplanned extras. In-room minibars have a complement of fun little "just because" items: wax lips, yo-yos, candy necklaces, Silly Putty, and Etch-a-Sketch boards. Turndown service offers surprises as well. One night there might be a Tootsie Roll on the pillow, the next a pack of Pixie Stix and, if guests are lucky, the occasional Illinois state lottery ticket.

Guests staying at a Walt Disney World hotel who are also scheduled to take a Disney cruise experience a preplanned value added that creates a lasting impression. The morning guests check out of the hotel to embark on the cruise, they are asked to leave their packed bags in their rooms and hold onto their room keys. When they arrive on ship, they discover their room number is the same as in the hotel, their luggage is already in the room, and they can use the same key. The very definition of a seamless service experience.

Other common preplanned value-addeds include:

- Breaking shipments into customer-specified portions rather than giving them standard take-it-or-leave-it lot sizes.
- Timing shipments to arrive when the customer wants them to arrive, not simply when it's convenient for your carrier.
- Changing billing dates and forms to fit the customer's systems.
- Making product modifications to fit customer needs and peculiarities.
- Applying special discounts to long-term preorders or volume purchases.
- Adding features like free Wi-Fi access in hotels, coffee shops or restaurants, or providing free car washes—and placing an ice-cold bottled water in cup holders–for cars serviced at dealerships.

## Eight Times to Include Value-Addeds

1. *For the good, solid, steady, no-complaints, no-noise customer.* Unspectacular, uncomplaining, salt-of-the-earth customers are often the most neglected. It's easy to take them for granted. It isn't easy to replace them with similarly good-natured people. If you do business with North Carolina-based Wilson Fence Company, expect to receive a letter beginning, "All too often, we do business with nice people, such as yourself, and then go on as if nothing had ever happened or without giving the customer a second thought. We would like to take a few minutes out of a busy day to personally thank you for your business."

2. *For the customer who has done you the favor of complaining.* By bringing a real or potential problem to your attention, complaining customers are giving you a chance (1) to regain their loyalty and goodwill, and (2) spot and fix problem areas in your service system that other customers might suffer with in silence. We know one CEO of a hotel chain who sends a personal "Thank you for bringing it to my attention" note to any customer who complains via comment card, letter, or phone call.

3. *For a new customer who has just placed a second order or increased the level of business they are doing with you.* One printing company we've worked with doesn't take new business as its due. New customers receive a special information packet, hand-delivered by the store manager, along with a gift jar (embossed with the company's address and phone number, of course!) filled with candy. Is yours empty? Let 'em know—they'll refill it when they deliver your next printing job.

4. *For a customer who has thanked you.* When someone goes out of their way to express their gratitude for something you've done in the course of your business relationship with them, you have a tremendous opportunity to deepen and strengthen the bond by responding in kind. A good friend wrote to Ralston-Purina to let the company know just how much her cat enjoyed Purina Cat Chow—Tabby wouldn't even touch other brands, would actually pick out the Purina pieces

and leave the rest if her owner tried to mix two together. A few weeks after writing, the cat owner received a thank-you note— and a coupon. She was surprised, but she shouldn't have been.

5. *For a customer who has been through a difficult time.* When things don't go smoothly, but your customer hangs in there with you, or when a loyal customer has learned the true meaning of Murphy's Law, a little "something for nothing" and corporate TLC is clearly in order. A woman who regularly shopped Stew Leonard's Connecticut dairy store went home empty-handed one evening when the computerized cash registers crashed. She couldn't wait for the system to come back on line because that evening was her husband's birthday, a fact she shared with a store manager when she called to off-load a little frustration. In short order, a Stew Leonard's station wagon pulled up outside her home with her groceries— and a cake with the frosted greeting "Happy Birthday from Stew and the Gang."

6. *When going out of your way will prevent a customer from having a problem.* Consider the Hairy Cactus Nail Salon in Cincinnati, Ohio, a full service salon that also provides manicure services. Understanding that time is money and that many a woman has ruined her not-quite-dry nails immediately upon leaving the salon, the Hairy Cactus came up with a simple but creative solution. Employees take the customer's purse and keys, open the salon door, escort her to her car, open the car door, put her belongings securely in the car, start the car, assist her into the seat and then watch her go safely on her way with not a chip or smudge to be seen.[1]

7. *For a good customer who has the potential for bringing you new customers or increased business.* Word-of-mouth advertising is more persuasive than any other kind. It's absolutely permissible to put words in the mouths of customers whose endorsement of your services can serve as a significant professional reference for your business. Adding a free car

[1]Ron Zemke and Chip Bell, *Service Magic: The Art of Amazing Your Customers* (Dearborn, MI: Dearborn Financial Publishing, 2003), p. 165.

wash to a tune-up for Mr. Jones makes good sense for the local Flying Flivver dealership—especially if Mr. Jones is the purchasing manager for ABC Widgets and the person who buys ABC's company cars.

8. *Anyone for whom you feel like doing a "good deed."* Sometimes giving a little value-added service just makes you feel good, regardless of whether or not it directly affects future business. So like the Nike ads say, "Just Do It!" Don't overlook your internal customers—your people—in the value-added process. At McGuffey's Restaurants in Asheville, North Carolina, employees receive ABCD (Above and Beyond the Call of Duty) sweatshirts when they provide unexpected pluses to restaurant customers.

We view "Going the Extra Mile" service as an honor—not an obligation.

—Hal Stringer
President, Peerless Systems, Inc.

# 17

# Make Recovery a Point of Pride . . . and a Focal Part of Your System

The true test of an organization's commitment to service quality isn't the stylishness of the pledge it makes in its marketing literature, it is the way the organization responds when things go wrong for the customer.

—Ron Zemke
Father of Knock Your Socks Off Service

All around the country, front-line service people are having to deal with customers who experience service failure. It's not their fault, anymore than it's the customers' (although it's worth repeating that about 30 percent of all problems with products and services are indeed *caused* by customers).

No service system is, or ever will be, 100 percent perfect. Sooner or later, something will go wrong. When it does, how your front line responds not only can make the best of a bad situation, but it can actually turn disappointment into customer satisfaction—sometimes even into customer delight! Hence the term *recovery*.

Recovery isn't simply about doing the right thing for your fellow human beings, it also can add dollars to your bottom line. A series of studies by TARP Worldwide found that when aggrieved customers had their problems satisfactorily resolved in quick fashion, they were more likely to purchase additional products than even those customers who experienced no problems with the organization to begin with. Research at Minneapolis-based National Car Rental found an 85 percent chance that a satisfied customer would rent again from National and a *90 percent* probability that a customer who experienced great service recovery would rent again.[1]

Home shopping service QVC Inc. understands how good recovery can help cement customer loyalty. A few years ago the company was selling NFL team rings at a record pace, primarily to wives buying them as Christmas gifts for husbands. But when QVC's guarantee to ship all rings before Christmas fizzled, the company knew it had to go beyond simply crediting customers for their purchases, as many other companies might have done. Resourceful employees remembered there were some high-quality NFL team jackets in the QVC warehouse, so the company matched them against ordered team rings and mailed them before Christmas—at no cost to customers.

Customer-centric organizations understand that solving customer problems swiftly and skillfully is more than a loss leader—it can contribute directly to revenue growth and profitability. At a minimum, good recovery is one of the best tools at your disposal for improving customer retention. However, the impact of poor recovery goes far beyond the loss of a single customer. The salesperson or customer service rep who dismisses a complaining customer with an "I can't help you, that's our policy," positions the company to lose dozens, if not hundreds, of potential customers. As ample research over the past 20 years has shown, unhappy customers go out of their way to tell as many people as possible about their bad experi-

[1]Jean M. Otte, corporate vice president of quality management, National Car Rental System, presentation to the MN Chapter, Society of Consumer Affairs Professionals in Business, June 8, 1992.

ence—and the potential audience for these tales of woe has grown exponentially with the advent of e-mail, online discussion boards, and blogs.

## Recovery Defined

Service recovery includes all the actions your people take to get a disappointed customer back to a state of satisfaction. Like the hospital staff or doctor nursing a sick patient back to health, service recovery is returning the customer "back to normal."

But great service recovery does not happen by luck, or solely by the interpersonal skills of your front-line people. Effective service recovery is planned and managed. It's a system that has to be designed and used just like any other system in your business. And your people have to know how to make it work on the customer's behalf.

You may be asking yourself, "Is this service recovery stuff something we even need to talk about?

Why not just put our energy into doing it right the first time? And, besides, maybe talking about mistakes will cause mistakes to happen more often—sort of a Pygmalion effect. Shouldn't our goal be zero defects? Shouldn't we accentuate the positive and eliminate the negative, as the old song used to advise?"

If service were always (or even mostly) perfect, we wouldn't need to talk about it. But it isn't. Service is neither designed nor delivered in a hermetically sealed room, where no contaminants can get into the process. It happens on the sales floor, in checkout lines, over the phone, on e-commerce sites, with the involvement of third parties, and subject to the disruptive influence of everything that is going on around it.

Instead of shuddering at the very mention of a potential problem, it's far better to prepare your people and the systems they work with to handle those occasional shortfalls. Keep in mind that customers have very different and unique requirements for "what is good service." A small mistake that causes one customer to say "ah, no problem" can make another customer livid.

Over the last 20 years, we've spent a lot of time researching the whys and wherefores of service recovery. Consistently, we find six caring actions that combine to make service recovery systematic, memorable, and satisfying.

1. *Apologize.* The point is not to determine who's to blame. It's to solve the problem. If your customers have a problem, chances are they're not happy. The first step to problem solving is to acknowledge the fact that—at least in the customers' eyes—a problem exists. As Tom Oliver, a senior vice president of sales and service at FedEx once told us, "If the customer believes he has a problem, he has a problem. Period." So start by having your people tell them, personally and sincerely, "I'm sorry."

A 2005 "customer rage" study by the Customer Care Alliance of Alexandria, Virginia, found that only 25 percent of respondents with service problems heard "I'm sorry" from customer contact employees, while 59 percent said that's what they wanted to hear. And some 75 percent wanted an explanation of why the problem occurred, but only 18 percent received one.[2]

2. *Listen and empathize.* This is not the time to instruct customers in the finer points of what they should have done to avoid the problem in the first place. Customers resent being lectured to. What they mostly want your people to do right now is just listen. Listening and empathizing helps customers unwind, get it out of their systems, and feel they're talking to someone who really cares about taking care of things.

3. *"Fair fix" the problem.* After listening (so they know exactly what's at issue), your people can snap to and, based on customer information and suggestions, work to resolve the problem. Usually, what customers want now is what they wanted originally—and the sooner the better. At Chick-fil-A

---

[2]"2005 Customer Rage Study" Customer Care Alliance and the Center for Services Leadership, Arizona State University School of Business.

restaurants, for example, if a customer arrives home to discover he was given the wrong drive through order, an employee will personally travel to his residence to deliver the right one.[3]

4. *Offer atonement.* Your recovery system will earn high marks from customers if it includes, even symbolically, some form of atonement that, in a manner appropriate to the issue at hand, says, "I'd like to make it up to you." But atonement is more than simply the "it's on us" or "no charge" offer. The word symbolic is carefully chosen; it suggests that little acts of caring, when sincerely done, mean a lot to customers. Consider the atonement offered by Aurora Health Care of Milwaukee, Wisconsin when a patient who'd just moved out of state discovered she was overcharged on a bill. Remembering that the woman complained about having to call long distance to correct "their" mistake, the hospital's billing department included a complimentary phone card along with her refund check.[4]

Of course, the bigger the service breakdown—and the more valued the customer—the more impressive the atonement will have to be to restore aggrieved customers to a state of satisfaction.

5. *Keep your promises.* Recovery time is double jeopardy "where the stakes are doubled and the scores can really change." Your system has already failed once. If your people make promises they can't keep in trying to get your business back in the customer's good graces, it will be throwing gas on the fire. Employees need to know how to be realistic about what they can and can't deliver, and how quickly.

6. *Follow-up.* In a few days, or a few weeks, have your people check back to make sure things really did work out to your customer's satisfaction. That kind of thoroughness and demonstrated concern builds loyalty that can weather future storms—and helps set you apart from competitors.

[3]Chuck Salter, "Customer-Centered Leader: Chick-fil-A," *Fast Company,* October 2004.
[4]Ron Zemke and Chip Bell, *Service Magic: The Art of Amazing Your Customers* (Dearborn, MI: Dearborn Financial Publishing, 2003), p. 165.

## Inside the Mind of an Aggrieved Customer

Once you have a recovery system in place, you have to factor in three important modifiers that govern the process from the customer's standpoint.

1. *Customers have expectations for how effective service recovery should happen.* Of course, you cannot learn what the customer expects unless and until you ask, which means soliciting complaints. There's solid data on the value of that orientation. Remember that only about one dissatisfied customer in twenty-five complains. Yet complaining customers can actually become more loyal than customers who pronounce themselves satisfied . . . if they've been listened to and responded to in a way that says you want them to come back again, despite this momentary glitch.

What does this mean to you as a manager? It means looking at customer feedback as a gift. When you get complaints from customers, share the information at the front line in a positive, not punitive, fashion. Rather than seek to find a guilty party, show your people that your objective is to retain the customer. If you shoot the messenger, your front-line people will neither encourage customer feedback nor report to you the service problems they identify. *You'll never find your fail points until it's too late.*

What's more, whenever you receive a complaint you should see and hear not one whining malcontent but twenty-five valuable corporate assets assembled around your desk deciding whether they ever want to come back and do business with you again.

2. *When customers experience a service breakdown, they need to be fixed as well as their problems.* Relationships are built on trust. A bad experience with you hacks away at that trust and creates an expectation (actually, a dread) that the same thing will happen the *next* time, too. That's why you want your people to listen and empathize first, and only then begin to ask problem-resolution questions.

Make sure they know how to respond to the Smokescreen Principle. Complaining customers often start by throwing up an emotional, sometimes even irrational, smokescreen first to find out how serious you are about listening to them. If your people dismiss the ranting and raving out of hand as sheer exaggeration, they're missing the point. Customers aren't used to having someone listen when they complain. This is their way of testing how serious you are.

Understanding and sympathizing with a customer's emotional state when events veer far off their anticipated course is an essential first step to returning them to a state of satisfaction. It's at this point where right or wrong take a back seat, and when the customer's unique perspective on the problem must be heard, understood, and, if at all possible, honored.

If you pass the test and get past that smokescreen, they will calm themselves down to the point that you finally unearth the rational, logical stuff that is key to fixing the problem. The emotional stuff is not going to help you fix the problem. But unless and until you get through it to the real issues, there's not much you can really accomplish.

3. *Effective planning leads to effective service recovery.* Top service providers identify places in their delivery system where service predictably fails and customers are left disappointed. Airlines and hotels often overbook, trains and planes experience weather delays or mechanical problems, restaurants overcook meals, and DVD rental companies mail the wrong movies to customers. Smart organizations outline service recovery standards to provide front-line people guidance in how to handle the customer who has been victimized. Although every situation is somewhat unique, guidance and clarity of expectations can provide front-line people the tools they need to come off competent and confident to the customer.

When it comes to service recovery, remember the axiom, *At that point where the customer is most insecure or incensed, you want your front-line people to be the most competent and confident.* The more you're able to work out the details of that approach in advance, the more recovery success you're likely to achieve.

## Five Ways to Make Recovery Routine and Support Your People

1. *Eliminate barriers.* The more paperwork and policy your front-line people have to fill out, duplicate, circulate, and take care of, the less time they'll have to really listen to the customer and the longer it will take them to find solutions to problems that the customer will find satisfying.

2. *Train their response.* At no time will the listening and empathy skills of your front-line people be tested more than when they have to deal with an irate, dissatisfied customer. Give them training that helps them develop skills beyond simply smiling. They need to know how to listen, problem solve, and handle the stress of dealing with upset customers. It's vital to help them learn not to take things said or done by "customers from hell" personally and to encourage them to vent frustrations offstage, not in the heat of the moment when interacting with customers.

3. *Support and encourage.* Be quick to praise and slow to censure. As noted performance consultant Martin Broadwell said, "Front-line people need all the praise and encouragement you can give them. They get all the bullets anyone can take from the customers. Praise is the bulletproof vest. The supervisor has to be the one to give praise and give it generously."

4. *Separate praise and critique.* Nothing is more demoralizing to a front-line person than to have the boss say something like, "Pat, you did a nice job on that . . . *but* you should have remembered to . . ." The compliment is always lost in the critique, diluting the value of both and tearing away a piece of the front liner's self-esteem. When it comes to recognition, make sure to "ban the buts."

5. *Always back your people in public.* When customers come to you with a complaint about a person on your staff, listen openly and nonjudgmentally, thank them for bringing it to your attention—but avoid a black-or-white determination based on "right and wrong." Find out what needs to happen to make the customer whole. Take care of that. Then, separately,

calmly, and generally in private, meet with the front-line person involved. Treat mistakes as opportunities for problem solving and learning, not rebuke and punishment. Forgiveness fosters courage and builds faith that managerial support will be present in the face of the occasional error.

> When it comes to service recovery, there are three rules to keep in mind: (1) do it right the first time, (2) fix it properly if it ever fails, and (3) remember: there are no third chances.

> —Leonard Berry
> Marketing Professor
> Texas A&M University

# 18

# Reinventing Your Service System

The greatest invention of the nineteenth century was
the invention of inventions.
                —Alfred North Whitehead
                English Mathematician and Philosopher

One of the "luxuries" of being a manager is that from time to
time you can stop, step back, and watch the thing you manage
work all on its own, without you and without strings, mirrors,
rubberbands, or first aid. It just works.

One of the responsibilities of being a manager is to use
those rare occasions not only to admire, but to examine and
challenge the same well-oiled service machine you so proudly
manage. We think of that as a charge to continually find ways
to "reinvent" your service delivery system.

In some Knock Your Socks Off Service organizations, that
job is even formalized. At Walt Disney World they talk about
"imagineering." The Orlando theme park has a vice president
in charge of parking lots, for example, whose job it is, among
other things, to find ways to "reinvent" the "parking lot experience" for Disney World guests.

Why? Because the majority of Walt Disney World guests
arrive by automobile. Most of them with one to three subcon-
sumers in the backseat, many of them on the end of a several-
hundred-mile drive. All of them expecting to experience

131

"Disney magic" from the first moment of contact to the last—both of which occur in the parking lot.

So the vice president of parking lots spends time worrying about how the lot lines move; worrying about how many guests will leave their keys in their cars, their lights on, and their motors running; worrying about how many times the tram driver should repeat the name of the parking lot area where a group of guests was picked up—so they remember later where to get off the train to find their cars.

The constant questioning—asking "How can we improve this experience?"—has lead to some marvelous ways of changing a common, everyday experience.

- Employees now cruise the parking lots in golf carts, looking for cars with lights on and engines running—and leave "don't worry, we have your keys" notes for guests.
- Tram drivers repeat the pickup point three times—to give us all a better chance of remembering.
- And there is a full-service repair shop tucked into one corner of one lot so that if anyone needs help in starting the family Hupmobile or changing a tire, Disney can surprise them with a little no-charge assistance.

## The Four-Question Inventing Process

How can you reinvent the part of the delivery system you manage? It takes a lot of creativity and a strong belief that what you manage and how customers experience it are critically important to your overall business success.

To help you, we offer the following four-question "process" as a beginning. As you work through each question, keep in mind your customers' needs (the outcome they seek—the product) and their expectations (how they want their needs met—the performance).

1. *What emotions and feelings are likely to invite the customer back?* What is the memory you want your customer to

take away as a result of doing business with you? Stated differently, what do you want your customers' "love stories" ("gosh, I just love the way they . . .") to feature?

For example, suppose you're the owner or manager of a small hospital. Since your customers (patients and their families) come to the hospital mostly when they are sick, hurt, or scared, you want them to remember feeling "personally cared for and about" after they leave—as though they were the only patient the hospital had to care for.

2. *What other service provider has produced those emotions and feelings for you?* Think of any vendor, store, or organization that, by the way it served you, left you with the kind of memory you selected in the question above.

Over a couple of years, Chip was working with a client in Alexandria, Virginia. His favorite place to stay was the Radisson Plaza Hotel (now the Hilton Alexandria Mark Center.) Atop the elegant thirty-story property was their upgraded floor accessible only by guest key—their concierge level they labeled the Radisson Plaza Club. They consistently worked to make Chip feel very special and "personally cared for and about." On one visit, they not only had the room pre-assigned and a personal handwritten note on the dresser, but also had his name on the laundry tags in the closet and the matches in the ashtrays. On check-in, the bell stand attendant called ahead and someone put fresh ice in the ice bucket. They even put a bookmark at today's date in the *TV Guide*. A week later, they sent him a handwritten thank-you note. Impressed by a first stay, his second was even more memorable. It was obvious to him that they wanted him to feel welcomed back, like an old friend. It created a very strong sense of being cared for.

3. *What specific part of your service delivery system needs to be improved, changed, or reinvented?* Don't try to take on every aspect of service you provide to customers. When you're trying to improve the performance quality of your service, the more specific you can be, the better. (Just as you'd concentrate on Act Two, Scene One to fix a play, or turning the double play to improve a baseball team.)

At Netflix, the online DVD rental service, management is constantly on the prowl for new ways to improve the customer experience. That focus has led to a series of innovations such as creation of the *Friends* network, which allows customers an online peek at movies their friends have rented and whether they've given them the thumbs up or down; allowing single customer accounts to create two or more "profiles," so different members of a family (or a couple) can develop their own online "queue" of movies to be mailed out when current rentals are returned; and a feature that recommends new movies to users based on the customer's own reviews of movies they're rented before, not simply on types of movies rented in the past. Some of these customer-friendly changes came as a result of input from focus groups that Netflix holds every week.[1]

From personal experiences as overnight patients in a hospital, we found the wait and hassle of admitting stood out. The forms were long. The staff was highly efficient, but no one seemed very glad we were there. The sterile hospital room was about as homey as an army induction center—there was a television in the waiting room and pastel paint on the walls, but the setting was not particularly full of life. There were a lot of stations to visit, and they all seemed far from each other. Worst of all, virtually everything, from the hallways and the waiting rooms to the people in them, felt cold!

Sound like an experience crying out for reinvention? The key is to stand back and experience your system as an outsider would. Places for reinvention will cry out to you as well.

4. *How would the designer of your "great service memory" model (question 2) redesign the part of your service delivery system on which you focused (question 3)?* In other words, how would the Radisson's Plaza Club revamp hospital admitting to ensure that every patient remembered the feeling of getting "personalized care?"

---

[1]Jena McGregor, "High-tech Achiever: Netflix," *Fast Company*, October 2005.

We suspect a Radisson-designed admitting process would:

Simply verify the information already in computer memory instead of making us go through a long, laborious registration process.

Perhaps issue a special card (as at the public library) that not only would give access to a special parking lot or special lounge, but might even generate the paperwork while we parked.

Ask what we would like to be called during our stay, what magazines we wanted to read, what kind of music to pipe in on the radio.

Introduce the key people who would be taking care of us—doing so as if introducing them to a friend.

Alert the lab that we were en route so the attendant would be able to greet us, and by the name we'd asked to be called.

Remember we liked strawberry and not chocolate ice cream.

And since our "vitals" are in their computer, send a birthday card as a follow-up after discharge.

## A Fresh Look

The four questions in the previous section are tools to help stimulate your creative processes. They provide a way to help you shift your service paradigm—a new way to think about how service might be delivered to the customer.

Notice how many of the supposed improvements to the hospital admitting process outlined above involve people rather than process: personal greetings, individualized touches, care and caring that are only possible if the people in the system are making the system serve the customer, not vice versa. That's why your people are front and center in this analysis—and in service in general.

In the midst of the fun and appeal of inventiveness is one important caveat: Whatever is created or invented must be grounded in what your customers will value and what your people can deliver. Before implementing a new way to deliver

service, ask customers their reaction and involve your people
in planning and piloting the changes.
   That's how you "knock their socks off."

   The mind of man is capable of anything. Because
   everything is in it. All of the past as well as all of the
   future.

                                        —Joseph Conrad
                                        English Novelist

# Imperative 5
# Train and Coach

Learning is a way of life in Knock Your Socks Off Service companies. In the past, new employee training often consisted of nothing more than "watch John for a few hours, then I'll turn you loose on the customers." If employees made some little mistakes during their first few weeks, well, customers understood about breaking in new help.

That was then and this is now.

Today, a walk-in-off-the-street, start-tomorrow-at-full-speed match is unlikely. Your methods, policies, and procedures are unique. So is the way you want customers treated. As for asking your customers to tolerate on-the-job training—forget that!

Knock Your Socks Off Service companies routinely spend the equivalent of 3 to 5 percent of salaries training employees—experienced as well as new. Managers believe that keeping everyone on top of changes in technology, competition, and customer demands is critical to success and survival.

*Management support* is equally critical to success in Knock Your Socks Off Service companies. Employees need to know and be able to see clear evidence that you are behind them in their efforts. They need to feel sure that you are on their side, that even if they make a mistake trying to do a good job for a customer, you will applaud the effort, if not the outcome.

Employees need to see themselves as colleagues if not customers in your eyes. Your personal credo should be: "If you're not serving the customer, you'd better be serving someone who is."

# 19

# Start on Day One (When Their Hearts and Minds Are Malleable)

Coming together is a beginning. Keeping together is progress. Working together is success.

> —Henry Ford
> Founder, Ford Motor Company

In the olden days of training, we used to talk about "getting them before they have teeth" —bringing on new people whose ideas and attitudes were open and unencumbered by a lot of bad habits and experiences.

- At that early stage of their job tenure, they were much more likely to accept our rationale for doing things in a certain way.
- If, however, we waited months, even years, before we started to try to build their Knock Your Socks Off Service skills, we often had the same kind of challenge orthodontists face when patients wait until they are adults before trying to do something about a gap-toothed grin.

Today we are committed to the importance of starting employees off with more than just the right technical skills. Marcia J. Hyatt, former director of employee development for Minnegasco (now CenterPoint Energy) a natural gas distribution firm, said it well when we first interviewed her on the topic. "If we believe employees treat customers the way they themselves are treated," she said, "then isn't it critical that we are as careful about the first impression we make on new employees as we expect them to be of the first impression they make on customers?"

If you believe, as we do, that actions often speak louder than words, then it is critical that we think about the entire new employee orientation *process* as carefully as we think about the basic program's content. Just as with our customers, we have to manage our people's initial experiences with the organization. Those first Moments of Truth on the new job can set the tone for years to come; they can, in fact, determine whether the new employee has a long tenure with the organization or will have packed and departed in short order and been replaced by another in an unending succession of slot-fillers and seat-warmers.

What message do we send to the new employees who report for the first day of a new job, only to find their supervisor and most of their new peer group absent, out of town, in meetings, or otherwise occupied? What values are we communicating when we drop them off in their new cubicle, hand them a new employee manual on CD, and bury them with "administrivia" and benefits forms?

The message isn't that the organization views them as a valuable resource, it's that they are simply the latest warm body to fill a seat and are to be moved as cost-efficiently as possible down the orientation assembly line. Yet plenty of research shows how effective good orientation can be at reducing avoidable turnover of new hires:

- Companies that provide a well-structured, comprehensive orientation can reduce turnover by up to 50 percent within two years, according to a study by Deliver the Promise, a consulting firm based in San Anselmo, California. The investment needed to build effective orientation programs pales in comparison to the high costs of turnover, the study found.

- A study at a large computer company demonstrated that the time for new people to reach full productivity shrank from five months to three for employees who had been carefully oriented to the company in general and their job and department in particular.

## Traditions

Perhaps the best-known example of turning the new employee orientation program into a sophisticated process with far-reaching consequences is the Traditions course at Disneyland and Walt Disney World. Every new employee who goes to work "at the park" is a graduate, whether they're going to be wearing badges that say *Guest Relations* or simply operating a broom and a dustbin.

Traditions is visible evidence of the extraordinary care that Disney takes to make sure that new employees understand the culture, values, and expectations of the organization. In the Disney vernacular, the world consists of only two classes of people: the "guests" who visit the park and the "cast members" who work there. In the Disney approach, new hires get a rare dose of reality as part of the new employee orientation process. They're shown, in detail, how hot, tired, cranky guests are capable of behaving—and misbehaving—and given an introduction to the ways the organization expects them to handle that important part of their job.

An equally far-reaching, though less obvious, part of the orientation of new cast members is the way they are treated during the orientation program—and, indeed, the care with which the whole orientation process is structured. The Traditions program is carefully scripted and conducted in a comfortable, specially designed Traditions training room. Instructors are well aware that they are setting the tone for the way these new hosts and hostesses will treat guests when they make their first onstage appearances. They're upbeat but realistic, supportive but challenging.

Other organizations combine special treatment for new hires with an early dose of service-related training. At some Fairmont Hotel and Resort properties, employees arriving for their first day on the job have their cars valet parked or get vouchers for a free night's stay at a property. Others wear bathing suits during orientation to experience the spa's exfoliating showers and mineral baths. The on-boarding program, designed to help new hires experience what guests go through—and to make them feel like VIPs in those highly impressionable first days on the job—is a result of focus groups that identified "showing empathy" as a key way for Fairmont to separate itself from competitors.[1]

## Tips for Making Orientation Work

What makes a first-rate new employee orientation program tick? Human resource and training managers say some of the best programs share these features:

1. *They avoid the day one "information dump."* The last thing people want on the first day of a new job, when excitement is at its peak, is to spend most of it filling out forms and reading benefits information. Shrewd companies have new employees complete these administrative tasks and set up e-mail accounts and passwords in advance of their first day. Rather than bury new hires in paperwork they seek to maximize interaction with coworkers and bosses on day one, as well as familiarize them with the building layout. Some of the most successful orientation programs pair new employees with a "buddy" for the first few weeks to show them the ropes and help them begin building a social network.

Realizing that information overload is a real problem on day 1 and that retention of content is often low due to nervousness or distractions, more companies also are opting for a staggered approach to on-boarding. They hold a series of orientation meetings

[1]Jena McGregor, "Customer First Aware Profiles," *Fast Company,* October 2004.

over the first month or two of a new hire's tenure to focus on different topics, give people more time to digest material and to develop greater breadth of understanding about the organization.

2. *They make orientation the joint responsibility of human resources and line managers.* Specifically, the most effective on-boarding programs maintain that HR should take responsibility for communicating information of organization-wide, relevant-to-all-new-employees nature, whereas supervisors should concentrate on issues unique to the employee's workplace and job. The job-specific training typically starts a day or two after the initial HR orientation.

3. *They effectively manage the expectations of new employees.* Two industrial psychologists, Kenneth N. Wexley of Michigan State University and Gary P. Latham, a Seattle-based consultant, found in their research that new employees, particularly those in first jobs, often have unrealistically high expectations about the amount of challenge and responsibility they will have on the job. Organizations, they suggest, must make entry-level jobs more challenging or align new-hire expectations from the "get go." There is a good argument that this kind of realistic expectation setting should begin even before orientation, in the selection process. It should continue through their initial experiences with the supervisor once they start doing the job.

Wexley and Latham have data to support the wisdom of making anxiety reduction one of the goals of an orientation program. They report that in an experiment at Texas Instruments, several groups of new employees went through a special, six-hour question-and-answer, give-and-take, getting-to-know the company session, in addition to a traditional corporate orientation program. The focus was placed on understanding the "real ropes" of the organization and what to expect from boss and peers on the job the next day. A year later, they found that these employees had learned their jobs faster and had higher production and lower absence rates than did employees who had gone through a more traditional new-hire orientation.

## The Adoption Metaphor

The hiring process may be all about survival of the fittest, but as you move from selection to orientation it's important to leave the Darwinian mindset behind and begin thinking more in terms of *adoption*, or how you can best assimilate new hires into existing groups. Consider using the ADOPT acronym as a guide as you develop or tweak your orientation process for improved results:

*A*ffirm the new employee for making the decision to be part of your organization or team.

*D*ebrief the new employee for service insights. People enter your organization with "fresh eyes" that allow them to see things in your service delivery system that grizzled veterans might miss or discount as "part of the furniture." As the proverb says, a *guest sees more in an hour than the host in a year.*

*A*sking for new hires' input also sends an early message that you value their opinions.

*O*rient your new hires to the values, standards, vision, and norms of the organization, not simply policies, procedures, and benefits. People want to know what the organization stands for and how they should tailor their behavior to best support that mission.

*P*artner the new employee with someone from outside his or her work group to show them the ropes beyond their unit and act as a "big brother or sister" for a few weeks.

*T*ribe. Borrowing from a Native American tradition that gave young braves a special task or challenge to mark their readiness to join the tribe, identify an assignment or project that a new hire can perform that has special meaning and makes a contribution to the team. It's critical that there is real work ready and waiting for people after the "Hi, how are ya? Glad you're gonna be with us!" stuff is over.

"Nothing is more frustrating to someone full of enthusiasm for a new job than sitting around stacking paper clips," say researchers Wexley and Latham.

There is an old shibboleth: "Well begun is half done." When it comes to getting a new employee off on the right foot and tracking with your organization's service focus, well begun is a lot more than half done. It may well be the most important first impression you can make.

> An employee is never more focused, malleable, and teachable than the first day on the job.
>
> —Horst Schulze
> Retired President, The Ritz-Carlton
> Hotel Company

# 20

# Training Creates Competence, Confidence, and Commitment to Customers

Excellence is an art won by training and habituation.
We are what we repeatedly do. Excellence, then, is
not an act, but a habit.

—Aristotle
Greek Philosopher

Nothing good happens for your customers or your organization until an employee makes it happen. Whether those employees are meeting face to face with customers or worrying over systems in the bowels of the organization, it is their skill and effort that make the difference between a Knock Your Socks Off Service organization and wishful thinking. Developing, honing, and keeping a competitive edge on your people's skills makes strategic sense.

It's not surprising, then, that in "service successful" organizations, training and development of employees are seen as a never-ending process that includes formal and on-the-job training, guided experience, effective coaching, targeted performance review, and strong support for learning from the organization. These companies know that if they're going to boast of superior service quality in their marketing or advertising campaigns, they better back it up with a staff trained to deliver the goods.

Providing more and better training for your people can and does create a big advantage in the marketplace. According to one study, employees who receive formal job training reach "standard" performance levels faster (72 percent faster), create less waste (70 percent less), and are better at customer troubleshooting and problem solving (130 percent better) than employees who learn their jobs by the tried and true—and very inefficient—"sit by Sally and ask questions" approach. In addition, there is pretty good evidence that employees who receive a significant amount of training on a regular basis—between twenty and forty hours a year—stay with you longer and receive higher marks in knowledge, skill, and hustle from customers.

## Training in What?

Despite its importance as a competitive advantage, however, don't confuse training with mother love, chicken soup, or high octane gasoline. It is not the case that if a little is good, a lot is better. Relevance counts as much as, maybe more than, minutes. To be effective, training should support serving customers better, working smarter, or creating better outcomes for the organization.

There are four kinds of skills your customer contact employees need to do their jobs well: (1) technical skills, (2) interpersonal skills, (3) product and service knowledge, and (4) customer knowledge. *All* are critical to their success. *All* need to be addressed throughout each individual's career with you. Following are some tips for developing and honing those four crucial skill areas.

## Technical Skills

• *Technology.* Today's front liners need to be more technology savvy than ever before. For many service roles that means mastering Microsoft Office software, an ability to deftly navigate the Web and communicate effectively with customers via instant chat and e-mail. It also includes knowing the ins-and-outs of handheld technologies, copiers, scanners, fax machines, cash registers (if you are a retailer), and the telephones.

• *Implication.* Assume nothing about your people's knowledge of your systems. Even if they've worked with a similar technology, they haven't yet worked with your particular variation on the system theme. What they don't know can kill you with customers.

• *Paperwork.* They need to understand the purpose of your paper records and systems, not just which blanks to fill in with what letters and numbers, but what role customer histories, status, incident reports, data integrity, and privacy considerations, and forms filled out by or for the customer play in your system of information management. Any time that paper affects the speed, reliability, and personal attention provided to customers, your people definitely need to know your forms and procedures cold.

## Interpersonal Skills

• *People Skills.* We're hoping you hired your service people for their abilities to listen, understand, communicate, and relate with customers as well as their technical and product skills. No matter how good their specific skills may be, the more training, the more knowledge, and the more experience you can give your front-line people, the stronger their skills will become—particularly in dealing with the most complex or emotionally charged service situations.

The burden needn't fall on you alone. A wide variety of books, simulation-based e-learning programs, DVDs, audio

CDs, and low-cost seminars exist to remediate poor skills and polish competent ones toward mastery.

*Caution:* Training sometimes is met with resistance, especially when it is perceived as an attempt to "fix" problems people don't know or admit they have. Even experienced employees need their people skills brushed up from time to time—such training should be seen as natural and supportive, not a reaction to a deficiency.

• *Self-Assessments.* Give your people a mirror in which to view their current performance levels. Encourage employees who deal with customers on the telephone to record several conversations and evaluate them alone, or with the help of an experienced peer. Use videotaped role plays to let them see themselves as others see them. Pass along customer comments, the results of mystery shops, and your own analysis and observations in a direct, timely, and positive manner.

• *Teamwork.* With a little training in the proper way to give another person feedback (Chapter 27) coworkers can help each other brush up on person-to-person skills. *Do not,* however, make this a requirement. People are generally apprehensive about receiving a job skills critique, especially when there is a possibility that the news will be less than thrilling. It is a tough spot to put a peer or pal in. The secret is to separate performance from person. Focusing on the former builds up skills. Concentrating on the latter tears down self-esteem.

• *Self-Directed Learning.* Give experienced employees the time and space (a couple of hours a month and a conference room will do) to role play different customer situations with each other, share tips and tricks, and generally talk shop. Don't attend these meetings yourself. The goal is for your people to learn from and with each other. That can't happen in the presence of the boss, no matter how "unthreatening" you think you are.

At Cabela's, the seller of outdoor recreation items that has become a phenomenon in states where it opens new stores, much of the knowledge accumulated by the crack floor sales staff is developed by peer-based training. Cabela's salespeople are encouraged to borrow products for a month—be it a tent, canoe, or fly fishing rod—and ask the same questions a customer might pose in order to learn more about the items. After the field test is over, employees fill out forms detailing the products' "highs and lows" and then give a presentation to coworkers about what they've learned. The feedback is also entered into "item notes," Cabela's knowledge management system which in-store and call center employees can tap to answer customer questions faster and more effectively.[1]

## Product and Service Knowledge

• *Technical Aspects.* Customers expect your employees to know more about the products and services you sell than they themselves, as customers, do. That's not always the case, however, which is one of the prime reasons so many people prefer shopping by Web site or catalog to shopping in stores these days.

• *Competitive Aspects.* Customers also expect your front liners to know something about the products and services your competitors sell. The more knowledge and factual information (as opposed to sales hype and "fluff and nonsense") they can give your customers, the less need your customers will feel for comparison shopping.

• *Customer Buypoints.* Do your employees know what questions customers most frequently ask about your products and services? And how to answer them? Do they have a list or file of common complaints about your offerings and your competitors products? Training can help them better anticipate and address customer needs or expectations.

[1]Michael A. Prospero, "Leading Listener: Cabela's," *Fast Company*, October 2005.

## Customer Knowledge

• *Customer Profiles.* Your customer contact people in particular can never know too much about their customers, whether that involves the personal tastes of a consumer or the products and services of a business-to-business client. Your front liners should be helped to develop a "style" for asking questions about customers and to write down what they learn. Customers expect your people to "stay told."

• *Heavy Hitters.* Encourage customer contact people to create files on each of their five best customers, with notes on what they've learned about them. What common elements do they notice that are missing from other customers? Would nurturing those traits build business as well as customer loyalty?

## Where Training Comes From

Knowing your people should be trained and getting them trained are separate issues.

• If your organization has a training department that delivers the type of training your employees need, that's a big plus. But that doesn't mean you're free to give the responsibility to someone else and wash your hands of involvement. You are responsible for insuring that the right skills are taught and that they are applied correctly on the job. (For information on how you accomplish all that, stay tuned for the next chapter.)

• If you are in a small company, or one with no formal employee training department or system, you are de facto the training director, administrator, instructor, and facilitator, all rolled into one. You can, of course, pass some of the tasks to a senior or lead employee. However, it's not a "short straw" situation—training is too important to be done poorly or by people who don't want the responsibility. You and/or your trainer designate will need to learn how to do effective job instruction training, called "train the trainer" training. Local universities, community or junior colleges, and vocational/technical schools can provide you with such training or refer you to an institution that does.

Successful Knock Your Socks Off Service companies are not only great performers, but learning companies as well. Their people are encouraged to be knowledge sponges, sopping up new information at every turn. They know you never know where you'll find an edge, so they look everywhere and all the time. You should, too.

The expense of training isn't what it costs to train employees. It's what it costs not to train them.

—Philip Wilber
Retired President, Drug Emporium, Inc.

# 21

# Making Training Stick

The beautiful thing about learning is that no one can take it away from you.

—B.B. King
King of the Blues

You fought for a training budget. Scraped together travel and expense money from the paper clip and staples fund. Sent your two finest off to a big deal three-day conference in Florida on the secrets of big-time customer service. Now they're back.

"So how'd it go?"
"Okay."
"So, what'd you learn?"
"Oh, you know, the regular stuff. But boy, that Disney World, what a neat place!"
"I'll bet it is. So, you took a lot of notes and have a lot of new ideas to share at the next staff meeting, right?"
"Well, ah, we didn't know, you know, that you expected a lot of notes and stuff."
"That's okay. I'll bet you have a lot of materials to share from the presentations. What were there, eight, ten different sessions?"

"Well, ah, you see, we didn't make a big point of grabbing up extras or anything. We were sort of, well, absorbing the experience, you know."

What they probably absorbed the most was good old Florida sunshine. And who can blame them? Whether you are sending your finest to Florida or your newest down the block to the corporate training center, if you don't prepare them for the experience—and help them integrate what they'll be learning into their back-on-the-job behavior—you aren't getting the most of your investment in employee training.

## Send Them on a Mission, Not Just "Out on the Town"

You can't really blame an employee who goes off to a big deal conference in an exotic setting for confusing the opportunity to learn something new with a reward for doing a good job. Even a one-day seminar away from work can seem more like a holiday than a special assignment.

The "learn something new" agenda of such junkets will be much more likely to occur if you send your people off focused on what you want them to bring back and knowing why that is so important to you, and should be to them. Without that emphasis, and regular reinforcement of newly learned skills back on the job, the time and dollars invested in training will have little lasting impact on the performance of your staff.

Here are three things you can do to make sure the people you send off to training get the most from the experience:

1. *Make training a highly visible event.* Create a little hoopla. Whether the training will be attended by three or a hundred, make sure that everyone knows it is important to you and the organization. Hold a short meeting. Tell everyone who is going off to training why they are going and explain what will happen when they return and how everyone will benefit.

2. *Hold a pretraining "heart-to-heart" expectations talk.* Sit down with the employees who are going—one at a time—

and discuss your expectations of the training and of their participation. Specifically, discuss (1) what the training will cover, (2) why the individual employee is going, (3) why the training is important to the organization, (4) your assessment of the employee's strengths and weaknesses as they relate to the content and objectives of the training, and (5) how you will help them apply the new skill or knowledge when they return from training.

If participants are going to be expected to share their observations with others on their return, it should be made clear what form that presentation will take. "When you come back, I'd like you to do a ten-minute recap of the high points at the Thursday staff meeting" is a very different expectation from, "When you come back, I'd like you to present a two-day training program for the rest of us."

3. *Assign pretraining homework.* The last thing an employee scurrying to make plans for a two- or three-day absence from the job needs is homework. Just the same, preparatory readings, data gathering, worksheet preparation, and other training-related tasks can prime and focus the employee for the experience to come.

- *Will the program be about dealing with unhappy customers?* Ask the person going off to training to gather feedback from coworkers on the most challenging customer problems they face or the most difficult types of customers they encounter.
- *Is it a course on team problem solving?* Have attendees interview you, other managers, or fellow employees about the greatest barriers to improving customer satisfaction with the team. (The people conducting the training can help you to decide the best sort of homework to assign.)

## Welcome Them Back—and Help Them Fit In

The training experience may have been great, the time spent highly productive and stimulating, and the interlude just what the doctor ordered. However, if nothing different is happening "back on the job," the momentum will die. Quickly. It's a more common outcome than you might suspect—the single biggest reason, in fact, why training doesn't "take."

The environment your people come back to must encourage and support their use of the new information and skills. As a manager, you are perhaps the biggest part of that supportive environment. If you've prepared them for the program, you should have a pretty good idea what content was covered and how it can apply to the individual's job and the broader needs of your work group.

Often employees need help using what they have learned. This is especially true when only a small percentage of your people (or just one person) goes to training. Employees want to perform differently, but will need time, incentive, and practice to break old habits and make the new way of doing things second nature.

## Back "Home"' Again

Here are five things you can do to help smooth the transition from classroom or self-paced e-learning programs to real world performance.

1. *Debrief people when they return or complete the training.* It may seem as if we are recommending a lot of chatting. We are. Letting people talk about the new ideas, approaches, and skills they have been exposed to helps the transfer to the workplace while reinforcing the value you put on the new insights they've gained.

The discussion should be more than a friendly chat, however. It should be fairly detailed, and questions such as "How do you think we can use that here?" should play a big part. Let your people show you that they have indeed come back with something new and useful. Be lavish in your praise of the new learning and ideas and the effort the employee has put forth.

2. *Hold a show-and-tell session for the department.* Asking people to explain the training content to others helps

them solidify what they've learned. As every teacher can tell you, real learning takes place when you have to teach others.

*Caution:* Some people would rather stand naked in a snowbank than address a group, especially of their peers. Find a different way for these people to share what they've learned. For example, have them write a two-page report as an agenda item for an upcoming staff meeting or share copies of key PowerPoint slide handouts from the session.

If you expect participants to actually train others, as opposed to simply delivering a general briefing, then special "train the trainer" preparation might be necessary. Good training always looks simple and easy—and it is, for the participants. However, it's much more difficult to repeat second hand, as a generalist trying to mimic the performance of a training specialist.

*Caution:* You need to be ready to "protect" your impromptu trainers and their new ideas. Sometimes, other employees may try to "put them down" or upstage their presentation—a former peer who suddenly acquires highly visible and highly valued new skills and stature can seem threatening to those who "stayed home."

3. *Hold a skill drill or practice session for the newly trained.* We learn best by doing, but actual skill practice may be minimal in a training program because of the number of participants, the style of the presenter, or the inability to address specific concerns in a general session. If it is important to turn the new learning into strong habits of performance, then the sooner the effort starts, the better.

4. *Catch somebody doing something new and thank 'em for trying.* Making a new behavior an active part of an employee's skill vocabulary takes time and practice. It also takes feedback and encouragement. Particularly from you. Be sure you set goals for the use of the new skill: "I expect to hear you using those new closing techniques in all your phone selling efforts by the end of the month." Then follow up positively, with interest and encouragement, not officiously, with a stopwatch and a clipboard: "That sounded great, Lee. Keep trying

those different closing techniques and I'm sure that by the end of the month you'll be booking all sorts of new business."

5. *Hold a contest—a fun contest.* Don't let learning to apply a new skill become a chore. Make at least some of the effort fun and challenging. Introduce some friendly competition or a lighter touch to keep everyone upbeat and enthusiastic. If, for instance, people have learned the same ten "closing techniques for telephone sales," you might have a one-day contest (perhaps announced, but on an unscheduled day of your choosing) during which you monitor calls and track the use of the new skills.

Keep it light! Make the awards small enough to be able to give out lots of them and invent a few off-the-wall categories to keep things fresh and unpredictable: an award for "Most Closing Statements Uttered in a Single Sales Call." Another for "Most Convincing Closing." Yet another for "Most Sales Actually Closed." And one acknowledging the "Strangest Closing Tried When the Customer Didn't Have a Clue What We Could Do for Them." Then, at the end of the day, reinforce the learning points by having everyone who won an award repeat what it was they had said—regardless of the category it was awarded for.

> Your performance depends on your people. Select the best, train them and back them. When errors occur, give sharper guidance. If errors persist or if the fit feels wrong, help them move on."
>
> —Donald Rumsfeld
> Former Secretary of Defense

# 22

# Thinking and Acting Like a Coach

> Coaching subordinates isn't an addition to a manager's job; it's an integral part of it.
> —George S. Odiorne
> Father of Management by Objectives

The definition of "boss" begins to take shape in most of us long before we get to the job market. It starts with "father" and "mother," then progresses to "teacher," "principal," and "coach." It may eventually include "professor," "scoutmaster," or "drill instructor." By the time we get to the work world, most of what we know about "bossing" has been shaped by people on whom we were dependent and times when someone else had close to complete control over our immediate actions and longer term destiny. Small wonder that "boss" for most employees is a four-letter word!

## From Boss to Leader

Directing the performance of a service, rather than supervising the production of a product, calls for a different management orientation. "Leading" a service performance isn't directly leading in the sense of being that someone out front, with everybody else falling into line behind you. Rather, service man-

159

agement requires leadership skills more often associated with indirect management—coaching a team, teaching a skill, conducting an orchestra, directing a play. In high-performing service organizations, managers need essentially the same skills that coaches use to bring out the best in a performing artist or athlete.

## Clipboards and Whistles

The similarities between service managers in business and coaches in athletics and the arts are many—and worth exploring as you try to give yourself a frame of reference for your managerial actions and responsibilities. Like a coach:

* *You instill fundamentals.* Your people have to know how to play their particular roles or positions: what to do, and when, and how, what to say, and why. Where to be when the customer feeds them a cue or throws them a curve. And just as great actors and athletes know the necessity of constant practice, of "getting in the reps" (repetitions) that help them master the part they are called on to play, you have to keep your people focused on the task and constantly honing their skills.

* *You build teamwork.* The second baseman is one of nine players on the baseball field. The violinist sitting first chair is just one player in the orchestra. No matter how individually talented he or she may be, the overall success of the production, be it the playing of a baseball game or a Beethoven symphony, is judged by how well everyone plays together. You position your players. You have to make sure they know how their role interlocks with others on the service team. You have to keep them focused on both their individual performance and the overall success of the group; keep the group working together in harmony in competitive conditions that challenge each in different ways.

* *You evaluate and adjust.* Every team, every individual performer, starts with a "game plan." However, typically the plan can only prepare; it can't control play from start to finish. There are other variables, often outside anyone's control, that

have to be taken into account in the midst of the performance. Like a coach, a service manager has to know how and when to replace or reposition players, change the script, react to immediate needs, and anticipate circumstances that may be encountered in the next quarter or the next act.

• *You reinforce and motivate.* The coach's role is to plan and prepare, react and adjust, correct problems without destroying the player's self-confidence, and praise good efforts without giving the recipient of the "well dones" a swelled head. You can't play favorites and build a united team. You can't preach sacrifice and dedication and then go put your feet up while your people give everything they've got. Your words and actions set the tone for theirs.

• *You're on the sidelines.* When the manager walks onto the playing field in most sports, play promptly stops. It doesn't continue until the coach has returned to the dugout, or the bench, or the wings. Just as you can't direct the play from the balcony or run the game from the locker room, you have to position yourself as close as you can to the action so you can support your players without either getting in their way or being so far removed that you don't know what they need from you.

## Preparing for Success

Before they take the field or the stage, players have to have a good idea of what they're going to be doing and how their individual performances will combine into a cohesive group effort.

• In sports, that preparation involves knowing specific actions to take in specific circumstances—with a player on first, the shortstop throws to second base on a ground ball to get the double play; when there's no one on, the play is at first base.

• In the arts, there's a script or sheet of music to learn, often augmented by marks to hit when delivering a line or modifications to tempo and volume that provide subtle changes to the look and sound of the performance.

Business organizations prepare themselves in similar ways. At Disneyland and Walt Disney World, the young men and women who make the rides and attractions "go" work from carefully planned and memorized scripts, complete with exceptions, situational variations, and approved modifications—ad libs, in other words. They know where they're supposed to be, what they're supposed to do, including how to take charge of a potentially negative situation and turn it into a positive for their guests. Disney's service deliverers practice a performance art. And that theme runs through training and management at every level.

## Matching Performance to Coaching Technique

Since the performance of your people is your paramount concern as a coach, your style and actions have to change to respond to specific needs. Here are some ways to flex your style for maximum impact in different coaching scenarios:

• *When your people perform well.* The adage, "different strokes for different folks" is as true on the shop floor or in the call center as it is on the playing fields. When performance is superior and the performers are appropriately challenged, good coaches search for outcomes (or rewards) valued by each individual and adjust their managerial style to the styles of their people. The key is to understand your best performers well enough to identify the specific rewards they value and the techniques that work best for them. In many cases the incentives or perks that motivate them will be far different from what you assume.

• *When your people perform unevenly.* Every coach is faced with performers whose play ranges from great in some aspects or at certain times to only average—sometimes less than average—in other areas. The appropriate technique is to reward the great stuff and to encourage improvement in the "only average"-*but not at the same time.*

When up-and-down performers hear, "Lou, you're doing great on *this*, but you can do better on *that*," they often miss the kudos because their minds immediately lock on the "do better" part. Sometimes, in fact, they can interpret your compliments as a not-so-subtle bribe to get improvement—"I really want you to buckle down here, so I'll throw you a pointless compliment over there to disarm your resistance"—in which case, you risk losing the power of the reward and the focus on improvement. Separate the "reward" part from the "encourage" part, and you help your people glow *and* grow.

• *When your people hit a slump.* Not even the best performers can do their best all the time. Sometimes they hit a slump or a lull during which everything seems to go wrong. When that happens, remember the classic coach's axiom: "If I traded players every time they were off, I'd wind up without a team in a hurry."

Good coaches patiently communicate continuous faith in the performer, especially when the results have been off and pride, confidence, and self-esteem are at their shakiest. They focus on and reinforce "the fundamentals"—the good efforts that will eventually pay off: "That's the way to go, Ann. Keep that up and I'm sure your sales (or service ratings, or retention/problem resolution rates) will improve."

Much has been written about the power of the coach's expectations on performance. It seems clear that *demonstrated* belief in people can help elevate their performance levels. If you think people will succeed—because you've put them in a position to do just that—and you treat them that way, you're generally not going to be disappointed. The reverse is equally true: Expect the worst and you'll have a very good chance of getting it.

• *When your people try and fail (and* **they** *don't know why).* This condition calls for the coach to function as a mentor. The Greek poet Homer tells us that Mentor was the trusted counselor of Odysseus (Ulysses), under whose disguise Athena became the guardian and teacher of Telemachus, his son and heir, while Odysseus sailed away to fight in the Trojan War. Mentor was known for his wisdom and sensitivity. Consequently, the word today is used to describe "a wise and trusted adviser." The challenge of the coach-as-mentor is to communicate wisdom and experience without creating defensiveness and resistance in the performer.

There are many aspects to mentoring. One key is to give advice in a manner that allows it to be heard, minimizes defensiveness, and keeps accountability for improvement with the performer. A useful approach to achieving such a tall order is to *first* get the performer's permission to give advice and *then* provide the advice as an "I" statement ("If I were you, I would . . ."). That's less telling and judgmental than an authoritarian "you should, you ought to, you had better" posture. Most performers, especially those confident in their skills and accustomed to succeeding, resent being told what to do.

Managers sometimes bristle at the suggestion that they should solicit permission from their people before giving advice to them. Who works for whom here, they ask. (If you're seeing your employees as customers of your managerial actions, not subjects on a feudal fief, the answer to that question should be obvious.)

The rationale is twofold:

1.  The performer may actually know what to do despite your perception that he or she does not. *Unneeded* advice becomes *unheeded* advice.
2.  This way, the coach keeps control and accountability with the performer, avoiding the surly look that says, "If you're so dang smart, why don't *you* do it."

• *When your people try and fail (and **you** don't know why).* This condition calls for astute analysis before action. A careful assessment of the performer and the performance often reveals unsuspected gaps in some ingredient required for high performance. Many managers faced with performance problems react in knee-jerk fashion by ordering up more training for the troops, but skill or knowledge deficiencies are only one among a litany of potential causes for service breakdown on the front lines. Here are eight variables to consider in searching for gaps between the performance required and the performance being delivered.

1. *Role-Person Mismatch.* Reexamine whether the performer would be more successful in a different role or on a different team.
2. *Task Clarity.* Perhaps the performer is not clear on the performance you require. Would you bet your next year's salary that *your* view of their accountabilities and expectations matches *their* view of those key parameters?
3. *Task Priority.* Sometimes failure is due to the performer's perception that the performance you expect is not really of high importance. Does their view of what's important match yours?
4. *Competence.* Failure can sometimes be due to a skill deficiency. People can't do well if they don't know how. Training guru Robert Mager offers an easy test to determine whether you're facing a skill problem or a motivation issue: "Could they do the job if their life depended on it? If no, you have a performance problem. If yes, you may have a performance gap no amount of training can correct."
5. *Commitment.* Failure can indeed reflect a will deficiency. Low desire or a lack of motivation can erode performance to the point that you get compliance, but little commitment. Have you given performers a sense of ownership and control over the work they do? Do they know "why" what you expect is expected (the rationale of the task)?
6. *Obstacles.* Real or imagined barriers can interfere with good performance. To the extent that you, as the coach, can modify or remove them, you can free your people to perform better. If you empower them to remove barriers, you build an even greater sense of ownership and responsibility among your front liners.
7. *Reward for Failure.* Sometimes there's more reward for poor performance than good performance. People who get attention (however negative) when they do poorly and are ignored when they do well may stop doing well just to get a reaction. (If you've ever seen a

"worst performer" award become more cherished than the "best performer" award, you've seen the dynamic in action.) You need to catch people doing well, too.

8. *Performance Feedback.* Do you provide clear, rapid information that helps your people evaluate and fine-tune their performance? Is it useful and presented from a consistent perspective? Or pointlessly general and subject to weather vane swings in emphasis that can confuse and disorient your staff?

If analysis fails to produce a reasonable explanation for substandard performance and does not suggest a path to a solution, a sit-down counseling session—focusing on the performance in question, not the personality or psychology of the person involved—should be the next step.

• *When your people don't try (or try to fail).* The last condition of performance analysis is the most complex and carries a tone of "acting like a psychologist"—so tread lightly here.

This condition could be rooted in performer hostility—toward the coach, toward the team, toward the customer, or even inward, toward self.

It might be due to burnout—cumulative stress and the absence of emotional support.

Sometimes it occurs when people view the performance standards set for them as arbitrary or capricious, or believe that as soon as they settle in to one performance level, the standard will be raised again, systematically outpacing their capacity to keep measuring up.

If none of these scenarios is the case, and you have tried all the appropriate actions without success, only then should you resort to official reprimands to attempt to pull performance back up to acceptable levels.

Reprimands are designed to stop negative performance, but in such a way that performance can be improved *without* undermining self-esteem or leaving scar tissue. As Ken Blanchard, author of the *One Minute Manager* series of books, is fond of saying, reprimanded performers should respond by focusing on what they need to do to improve, not on how they were treated by the person delivering the bad news.

Most good books on discipline tell us that reprimands:

- Should be delivered in private.
- Should focus on performance rather than the person.
- Should be given with frankness, but not in anger.
- Should be appropriate to the infraction.

Good coaches do all of that and one more thing: They underscore the impact an individual's poor performance has on the team's performance. They know that it is far better to have people working hard to avoid letting down their teammates—or to meet their own high standards of performance—than making them sweat to impress their coach.

The game of human achievement is played with complex players, changing rules, and ambiguous measurements. The coaches we admire on the sidelines at Sunday's game or behind the performance of a talented artist or performer have much to teach us that's relevant for Monday's corporate game.

> I spend most of my time thinking about what will motivate players.
>
> —Pat Riley
> Head Coach, Los Angeles Lakers

# Imperative 6
# Involve and Empower

*Involvement* is the enfolding of an employee in the decisions and the work of the organization. Think about it. If two heads are better than one, what could happen if *everyone* who works for you focused their brain power on your biggest problem?

Involved employees willingly think beyond the rudimentary features of their jobs and take on the role of problem finder and solver. However, involvement is a two-way tunnel. Employees who are encouraged to be part of a problem finding or problem solving or new idea effort expect to have their ideas taken seriously. Any hint that an involvement effort is employee relations window dressing quickly kills commitment.

*Empowerment* is working *with* your people to enable them to perform beyond simple rules—to act intelligently, not out of habit, routine, or fear. Empowerment is neither a gift nor unlimited license. It is an act of development, a matter of helping employees feel an increased sense of control over their work, decisions, and environment in general.

"I'm sorry sir, I just follow orders" is the stock answer of an employee in a "don't think, just follow the rules" organization. "Let me see what I can do about that" is the signature of empowered employees working on behalf of *their* customers.

# 23

# Fostering "Responsible Freedom" on the Front Lines

Sooner or later you have to trust your people.

—James Barksdale
The Barksdale Group

Bill had worked during lunch with the client so he could get back to his hotel to change clothes for an important dinner meeting in a nearby town. He was staying on one of those fancy upper floors, concierge level as they liked to call it. By 4:30 P.M., he'd made the quick change and realized he had almost half an hour before the client was to pick him up. Having skipped lunch and with dinner still several hours away, he realized he was starving! Not to worry, he figured. The concierge floor had a lounge area that provided small sandwiches and spicy meatballs to guests. A quick snack and a soda would tide him over.

Alas, Bill had not figured on the prickliness of the guardian of the concierge lounge. "Hors d'oeuvres," she informed him with all the pointless authority of the petty bureaucrat she apparently aspired to be, "are served from 5 P.M. We're not ready to open yet."

Over the rumblings of an empty stomach, Bill started to explain his plight. "It's wonderful that the hotel is willing to lay out such a nifty spread," he said. "Yes, he certainly understood the rules," he acknowledged. "But since the chafing dishes are obviously already hot and full, and the plates and silver ready and waiting, we could surely jump the gun by a few minutes, right?"

"Sorry," came the reply in a tone of voice that made it clear she wasn't. "I have my rules. You'll just have to miss out, I guess." And with that, three very bright, positive days in that hotel turned ugly brown, done in by an employee more concerned with policies and procedures than serving and satisfying customers. Bill hasn't been back to that hotel since, nor will he be stopping by anytime soon. He's taking his business someplace else these days.

Was the woman genuinely nasty, mean, and awful? Or was she just another unempowered employee, afraid all heck would break loose if she sidestepped policy and passed out a single meatball 20 minutes before the posted time? It's hard to know from the here and now. However, we do know that genuinely empowered front-line employees are the ones who most genuinely delight in shaving this corner and bending that minor rule to make a customer happy. And the managers of genuinely empowered people are the ones most prone to aid and abet them at every turn.

## What Empowerment Is—and Is Not

Yet many managers have an ongoing and often irrational fear of the "E" word—*empowerment*. They have heard one too many speaker and seen one too many film suggesting that "empowered employees" are simply inmates placed in charge of the asylum, set forth unbounded by rules to "do whatever it takes to make the customer happy."

What are they afraid of? The predictable things, of course: that employees who are turned loose will give the store away to conniving customers; that they'll try to buy customer satisfaction at the expense of profit, ducking the hard and nasty work of telling a customer no when that's the right (or only) answer.

Our experience (and we've yet to encounter anyone whose own experience doesn't agree) has been that customer service people seldom do such things—*if* they are well trained and managed, and if empowering them is a process rather than a pronouncement.

Empowerment is the self-generated exercising of professional judgment and discretion on the customer's behalf. It is doing what needs to be done rather than simply doing what one has been told to routinely do. From the manager's perspective, empowerment is a key element in the process of releasing the expression of personal power at the front lines. It is the opposite of enslavement.

Empowerment is not a gift one gives to another, because personal power is already present within the individual. To the contrary, personal power is released when managers and supervisors remove the barriers that prevent its expression. The distinction is important because it focuses us more on what we take away from the system than what we give to our people (Figure 23-1).

What does empowerment look like? An empowered act, by definition, is exercising initiative beyond or outside the

| Empowerment Is NOT A Gift | | |
|---|---|---|
| • Something you encourage | NOT | • Something you give |
| • Congruence | NOT | • Compliance |
| • Consistency | NOT | • Conformance |
| • Accepted | NOT | • Assigned |
| • Partnership | NOT | • Parental |
| • Values Oriented | NOT | • Rules Oriented |
| • Right Things | NOT | • Easy Things |
| • Appropriately | NOT | • Correctly |

**Figure 23-1.** Empowerment Is Not a Gift.

conventional norm. Confidently following the policy may be appropriate, and quite frequently satisfying, to a customer seeking nothing more than the standard offering. However, it is not an empowered act.

Empowerment kicks in when the customer's long-term loyalty is at risk because of an unforeseen problem or unanticipated request. It's also at work in the little value-addeds that can make the most ordinary of service transactions extraordinarily memorable and positive for the customer.

## E Is for Excellence

Service quality research over the past two decades has shown empowerment to have many benefits:

• An empowered employee can more effectively manage the customer relationship and turn superficial contact into a true partnership than one who must constantly balance instincts to "do the right thing" against the fine print of a policy and procedure manual.

To the customer, an empowered employee is a powerful commentary on the whole service orientation of the organization. Nothing sets an upset customer's blood boiling faster—particularly one who's already invested significant time and energy trying to solve a problem or get an answer—than hearing a front-line employee say, "I'll have to check with my manager." Empowered people send a message that a business truly does put customers first. Unempowered people tell customers that the organization has so little regard for its customer contact staff that managers are unwilling to give them the power to make customers happy.

• To the employee, empowerment has significant effects on self-esteem and morale and carries a strong message about management's priorities and behavioral style. As University of Maryland's Benjamin Schneider has repeatedly demonstrated: *Treat your people like gold—or dirt—and they'll treat the customer accordingly.*

Today, more than ever before, we want and need people whose sense of responsibility to serve the customer takes precedence over a jumble of organizational red tape. It's up to managers to strip away the layers of organizational inertia that have calcified over the years so people can do that in a professional way that benefits themselves, their customers, and the organization.

## Making It/Letting It Happen

"How do I empower my employees?" is a question as flawed as "How do I motivate my employees?" It may be even *more* flawed, since eliminating "boss control" is at the core of empowerment and the "how do I" part of the question, no matter how well intended, still reeks of "boss control." So where and how does real empowerment start? What can a manager do to see that it starts at all? A short story will help explain the forces at work.

A patient at Aurora St. Luke's Medical Center in Milwaukee lost an inexpensive but favorite pair of sneakers during his stay. Housekeeping, after learning of the man's complaint, concluded that someone had mistakenly thrown out the sneakers and was quick to offer a heartfelt apology. Not good enough. Offers to pay for the patient's sneakers also were not satisfactory. The patient wanted *those* sneakers.

At that point, the traditional response would likely have been a diplomatically insipid form letter saying something along the lines of "Thank you for bringing this matter to our attention. Your satisfaction is our only goal. If we can ever . . ." and making it clear that reasonable people had done all that could reasonably be expected over a pair of sneakers. End of story.

Instead, a young part-time housekeeper who had been involved in some of the telephone calls over the incident took over. Acting on his own and not on a managerial directive, he got a detailed description of the sneakers from the patient, left work, went to a store, and, using his own money, purchased a replacement pair of identical shoes.

The patient was surprised. And elated. And the young part-time housekeeper? He received St. Luke's first ever award for the most meritorious act of empowered behavior. It's called the Golden Sneaker Award.

That's what empowerment looks like. No one "gave" permission for the housekeeper to leave work to go buy sneakers. He exercised the personal power he had always had on the customer's behalf. He thought first and foremost about what was really at issue—a pair of shoes, not assessing internal blame or hewing to the strict interpretation of hospital policy over patient claims of lost items.

By choosing to celebrate his action on an organizational scale, managers at St. Luke's sent the message that this kind of behavior is not aberrant or suspect. It's an example of what everyone can and should do if the hospital is to continue to attract patients.

Of course, not all your employees will be as eager as the St. Luke's housekeeper to go above and beyond to satisfy customers. As much as they might dream of taking such bold actions, the reality is that when push comes to shove, many of your people would rather someone simply tell them what to do rather than devising creative solutions themselves. Others might resist because of "doing more with less" work environments—they feel like their work plates already overfloweth and replicating the housekeeper's actions doesn't feel plausible given the strict productivity and efficiency goals they're expected to meet.

So how can you get more front-line employees to take the initiative with customers? One way is to treat them more like partners than subordinates. Position-based power management—the "because I said so" type—is fast becoming the last resort of the inept. One of the quickest ways for employees to learn whether they are really empowered or not is to make a visible mistake in the name of pleasing customers. If the error is met with rebuke and punishment—if the empowered decision is denigrated by a superior—it sends quite a different message than if the manager see it as an opportunity for learning or improved problem solving.

That doesn't mean you should give employees unlimited license to please customers—some elastic guidelines are still required. The manager who says "just do what you think is best" is more likely demonstrating abdication (or fatigue at the end of a long work day) than empowerment. The goal should be to give your people "responsible freedom" defined by clear, real-world examples of how they might fix customer problems in a variety of service situations—without first coming to the boss for the green light.

Today's new partner-leaders focus less on sovereignty and more on support with controlling behaviors taking a back seat to a coaching mindset. If empowering people truly is your goal, it's a leadership model you would do well to emulate.

> Our people in the plants are responsible for their own output and its quality.
>
> We expect them to act like owners.
>
> —Ken Iverson
> Author, *Plain Talk: Lessons from a Business Maverick*

# 24

# Removing the
# Barriers to
# Empowerment

The customer walked into a crowded fast-food restaurant and
ordered a sandwich, small fries, and soft drink to go. Told
there would be a short wait, he stepped aside while the
counter clerk waited on others. By the time half a dozen customers had worked their way past him, he was losing patience. Fast food, eh?

Finally, his slow burn now beginning to fog nearby windows, his take-out order was ready. As he stepped to the
counter, prepared to provide a little direct feedback on his service experience, he was met with his bag, a confident smile,
and a surprise: "I'm very sorry you had to wait," said the high
school student who had taken his order. "I know you're in a
hurry. Because you had to wait, I gave you a large order of fries
instead of a small one. I hope you'll come back real soon."

Anger? Gone. Impression? Positive. What kind of place is
this, where seventeen-year-olds can diagnose and disarm upset

customers on the spot, on their own and apparently with no need to protect the return on the restaurant's potato investment?

It's a Hardee's, actually. One of thousands where they teach people, "Don't fight, make it right." The extra fries didn't disappear into the inventory ozone. They were accounted for—on a pad of "Saved Customer" forms. Built into the Hardee's approach to fast food is a recognition that customers have plenty of alternatives these days and a conscious decision that an extra helping of fries, a larger soft drink, or an occasional cookie on the house is a relatively inexpensive but very effective way to make sure they come back again when things don't quite turn out right.

Notice that the responsibility for turning that corporate mindset into action rests squarely on the shoulders of the seventeen-year-olds (and thirty-four year olds, and sixty-three year olds) who work the counters and the drive-throughs, typically at or near minimum wage pay scales and without benefit of a couple of years in an MBA program. How does Hardee's give that sense of empowerment to those kind of front-line workers?

It doesn't. The power is already there with the people who tally the orders and bag the food and fill the soft drink cups. What Hardee's has done is remove the barriers that prevent front-line service professionals from taking action when their own observations of what their customer is experiencing tell them that action is indicated.

If *your* employees come to work with adequate power to act with responsible freedom, what prevents this power from being used? Something obviously gets in the way. The key to the manager's role *vis à vis* empowerment is found in understanding the barriers and then working to remove them.

The task at hand is to encourage the directed use of responsible freedom on the customer's behalf. The challenge is one of coordination: getting employees to act with responsible freedom *and* in ways that benefit the customer plus the organization. It's not an impossible quest. Here are four consistent reasons that front-line employees fail to act in empowered ways—four "P" words that sum up the ways organizations have in the past effectively said no to their people's empowered instincts: no purpose, no protection, no permission, and no proficiency.

## No Purpose

People will act with power if they experience a greater purpose in their work than simply the day-to-day task. For frontline employees to act with extraordinary zeal, they must believe that it is their purpose to "make a customer happy" or to "make the service or product work like it's supposed to." Purpose is the "Oh, so *that's* why I'm here" explanation that energizes and motivates.

FedEx founder and chairman Fred Smith tells his employees, "We transport the most important cargo in the world—an organ for a vital transplant, a gift for a special ceremony, a factory part that may have halted a major enterprise." Employees take that service vision seriously, as evidenced by the actions of FedEx courier Joe Kinder during a raging snowstorm. The storm had shut down the city, but Kinder had an important delivery—visas for a couple traveling to Russia to adopt their son. The weather prevented the package from arriving on the expected day, and the couple was due to leave for Russia the next morning. The situation was dire; without the visas the couple couldn't adopt the child.

With things looking bleak and the service promise echoing in Kinder's mind—"precious packages have to be delivered on time"—he decided to take action. After some investigative work Kinder tracked the package down, and despite dangerous road conditions drove out to the couple's home and delivered the visas to an ecstatic response. His actions allowed the couple to leave on time and bring home their new son.

Here's how you can instill a sense of purpose in your own work group:

1. Talk about your vision often. Focus on what you want the organization to *be*, not just what you want it to do.
2. When communicating expectations, describe the "whys" as well as the "whats" and "whens."

3. Recognize corporate heroes by "telling their stories"— the details of their special accomplishments that become examples for others to follow.
4. Live the mission by making sure your daily actions are consistent with the purpose you've set for your people. Examine how you spend your time, what you show excitement about, what you worry about. Your actions telegraph your true priorities to those around you.

## No Protection

Jerry Harvey, author of the *Abilene Paradox*, maintains that resistance to change is a myth. "It is not change people resist; it is the prediction of pain over which they have no control." says Harvey. A consistent barrier to employees acting with power is their prediction of pain: "If I make the wrong decision, no safety net will catch me."

As a manager, you need to reduce the risk factor your employees may associate with empowered actions. Even if it makes you tense up and cross your fingers to think of them out there on the high wire, your job is to reinforce their courage and commitment so they go out and try again.

What you can do:

1. *Examine your procedures.* Employees may feel unprotected due to past practice. Punish an infraction and, if you are not careful, you will create a precedent. Are employees clear on the difference between what is a "thou shalt not . . ." and what is an "it would be better if you didn't . . ."?
2. *Recall the last few times an employee made an honest mistake.* Was the error met with reproach and guilt, or was the mistake treated as an opportunity for learning and growth? Is forgiveness for mistakes directly spoken or just tacitly implied?
3. *Are employees publicly given the benefit of the doubt?* If your people were interviewed by an outsider, would they say they received more coaching or more cri-

tiquing? How many times do employees get praised for
gallant efforts that failed to pan out as planned?
4. *Are employees commended for seeking assistance
   from others, including those in superior positions?*
   Managers should be a helpful resource on call as
   needed, not a troll lurking under an organizational
   bridge that people fear disturbing for the havoc it might
   wreak upon them.

## No Permission

As a manager, you need to continually and explicitly give
your people permission to act on the customer's behalf. It's
dangerous to assume that employees will just know what they
are and aren't allowed to do—or even that they'll believe you
the first time you say, "Yes, you can." Employees have been
hearing managers say no for generations from their experiences as customers and their on-the-job encounters.
Empowerment takes some getting used to. As an executive of
a newly formed "baby bell" once told us of how business
changed following the breakup of AT&T: "Overnight, we went
from a business in the business of saying no, a public utility,
to a business that had to learn how to say yes."

Organizations that turn front-liners loose to solve customer problems and regularly solicit their ideas for boosting
service quality often reap impressive benefits. Some of the
best notions for improving service come not from the strate-
gists sitting on mahogany row but from those who spend most
of their days listening to customer problems and concerns.
Tapping into their collective experience makes good business
sense—most of your service reps will speak to more customers
in one day than executives will in a year.

While the tendency is to think these suggestions will run
toward the cost-prohibitive or pie-in-the sky, our research
shows that when front liners are asked for improvement ideas
most are as careful to consider costs of implementation as they
are impact on customer satisfaction. And by regularly involving them in this way, you create a stronger sense of ownership

and send a message that their experiences and opinions are valued—two factors research has shown to boost morale and retention rates.

At USAA Insurance, management regularly encourages customer service representatives to suggest changes that will improve the customer experience. One rep's recent idea to offer insurance premium billing that's timed to the military's biweekly paychecks (the insurer's core customer base) is just one of the many front-line suggestions the company has implemented over the years.[1]

What you can do:

1. *Take to heart a line on the menu in Asheville, North Carolina-based McGuffey's Restaurants: "The answer is 'yes,' what's the question?"* Apply that kind of thinking with your people. Model responsible freedom and measured risk taking by your actions. Where you lead by example, others will follow.
2. *Examine your reward and recognition practices.* Which is more valued: creativity or compliance? Being adroit and resourceful or being accurate and right? Who gets praised or promoted—and for what?
3. *Use "zero-based" rule budgeting.* If you eliminated all the rules, regulations, and policies attached to your employees' roles, and then added back only those that are absolutely relevant, would you be writing restrictions long into the night?

## No Proficiency

"Knowledge is power," said English poet Francis Bacon. The capacity to find clever, resourceful, and creative solutions is the mark of a wise person prepared and empowered to go beyond the traditional, the familiar, and the ordinary. Training your people, not once but constantly, provides not just com-

[1]Jena McGrego, "Employee Innovator USAA," *Fast Company,* October 2005.

petence but wisdom. And whereas competence promotes confidence, wisdom fosters power.

The late author Malcolm Knowles told the story of a medium-size manufacturer of radios and televisions that realized the electronics industry was on the eve of a sizable transition from vacuum tube to transistor technology. The company began to train heavily—even in courses that would not be approved according to most tuition refund policies. When the industry began to change over to transistors, this company quickly grabbed the dominant market share in the electronic appliance world. The company is Sony.

One reason that Sony's top brass gave for the company's meteoric rise was learning. They reasoned that the more people learned, the better learners they would become and the more likely they would want to learn. Sure enough, Sony employees learned new transistor skills at a much faster pace than their competitors. In addition, the more they learned, the more empowered employees felt. They had the courage needed to risk exploring new techniques and alternative approaches.

What you can do:

1. *Emphasize proficiency.* Recognize and reward those in your work group whose performance stands out and by using them as mentors and team leaders.
2. *Be a lifelong learner yourself.* Again, the example you set is the one your people will follow.
3. *Develop a folklore of empowerment stories.* These are anecdotal evidence that communicates (1) that empowered actions should be taken and (2) specific examples of how it may be done.

Our employees probably make more decisions in the hallways than most companies make behind closed doors.

—John Oren
Managing Partner
Pinch Transportation Group

# Imperative 7
# Recognize, Reward, and Celebrate

Creating Knock Your Socks Off Service is a human endeavor. It happens when a group of people willingly and enthusiastically work together to create something none could accomplish alone. Human nature is a key factor. Understand it and respect it and it will work for you. Disregard it, ignore it, downplay its impact, and it will work against you.

The people who work for and with you want to do a good job. They want to work for an organization and in a department that is successful. They need something back in return. They need to know how they are doing: whether they are succeeding or failing, are average or exemplary, and what they can do to improve when improvement is needed.

They need to be recognized and rewarded for their accomplishments and their efforts—sometimes individually and
sometimes as a part of a group effort.

In addition, they need to be enfolded in something beyond
their own ability to achieve by celebration of the effort and
achievements of the corporate "all of us together."

# 25

# Recognition and Reward: Fueling the Fires of Service Success

Recognition drives the human engine.
—Leonard Berry
Texas A&M University

"Catch somebody doing something right today" is an admonition that succinctly captures years of managerial wisdom and a ton of behavioral science research. It has special meaning and import for the service management effort. If you want people in your organization to think and act in customer-oriented ways, seek out ways to catch them doing just that, and reward and recognize them for making the effort.

It is a reasonable and rational guideline, a precept hard to disagree with—and one more easily broken than kept. The biggest problem, of course, is that in the modern service workplace most managers seldom see more than a small sample of employee behavior, and therefore have few opportunities to personally catch employees, particularly front-line employees, doing *anything*—good, bad, or indifferent. You have to be prepared to use what you see and find ways to see more.

Research shows that many service employees leave their jobs simply because they feel unappreciated in their work. That makes finding small ways to show your people you value what they do each day in the name of pleasing customers one of the best—and most cost-effective—methods for reducing attrition levels and boosting performance.

Effective recognition and reward oil the wheels of willing cooperation and dedication to the job.

- *Reward* typically connotes money: salary and bonuses, cash awards, financial incentives, and other tangible payoffs in lieu of cash (though often chosen and presented in terms of their cash value).
- *Recognition* is typically less tangible, given for taking a little extra time with a customer, for going a step beyond nominal expectations, for caring about what the customer needs and expects to be done, and looking for ways to do it better, faster, smarter.

## From Practice to Program

Recognition and reward come in as many styles as there are recognizers and rewarders. Common approaches include:

- *High-Profile Formal.* Programs such as "Bravo Zulu" and "Golden Falcon" (Federal Express), "Service Star" (Chase Manhattan), "Customer Champion" (T-Mobile) and "Heritage Award" (Great Plains Software, a Microsoft subsidiary) come complete with detailed rules and objectives that everyone learns and set prizes, payoffs, and awards that everyone can strive for.

*Caution:* Make sure your recognition spotlight doesn't put employees on the spot. If someone doesn't feel comfortable standing up to take a bow, respect their wishes.

- *Low-Profile Formal.* Little rewards can be as effective as the big ones if they are used the right way. Nonmonetary awards possess the "trophy value" that cold hard cash doesn't;

while few people dislike cash and it provides a quick rush of satisfaction, the money usually disappears quickly and employees are left with nothing to remember their accomplishment. Lapel-style pins, plaques, framed certificates, and embossed business cards that list service awards are tactics common to service leaders. Others award good suggestions for new or better ways to serve customers with free video rentals, tickets to sporting or cultural events, courtesy time off, gift certificates, or points redeemable for merchandise at the company store. In one retail bank, the employee who submits the month's best idea wins a circulating trophy—a three-foot–high light bulb.

The trick is to avoid one-size-fits-all reward plans. Give employees a choice of awards so they can choose something that fits their tastes. One person's sporting event nirvana, for example, might be another's snooze-inducing "night that wouldn't end."

- *Informal.* A simple "thank you for your effort" note or a verbal "well done" delivered in front of coworkers are great ways of recognizing people. Style counts every bit as much as substance. A handwritten note from the CEO saying nothing more elaborate than "I really appreciate the extra effort you expended making the senior officers conference a success" is often more powerful—and certainly more lasting—than cash on the barrelhead. It's the sincerity and acknowledgment that count most to the recipient. Ditto for similar notes that you send to your front-line staff. In this day of ubiquitous e-mail, a heartfelt "thanks" note penned by hand can make a big impression.

## Avoiding Reward Pitfalls

You'll also want to ensure your reward and recognition efforts don't fall prey to the law of unintended consequences. Organizations and managers sometimes can do more harm than good in how they choose to design or implement recognition plans. Beware of these pitfalls:

- *Winner-Take-All Plans.* Competition is healthy in the marketplace but it can be demotivating in the workplace. Abandon employee of the month or other winner-take-all service reward plans in favor of those that recognize more people for the small things they do every day to please customers or assist coworkers.
- *Perception of Favoritism.* When peers have some say in the voting process for formal rewards people tend to see the process as more open, honest, and fair than if a manager unilaterally chooses award recipients. After all, who better to identify the service stars (and slackers) than those working alongside them on the front lines?
- *Lack of Immediacy.* Waiting for weeks or months after someone exhibits commendable behavior to reward it dulls the impact. Deliver rewards or recognition as close to the contribution or event as possible.
- *Same Old, Same Old.* Even the most inventive and unique awards grow stale and lose their impact over time. Survey your employees to make sure they still see your reward or recognition plans as appropriately motivating. If the answer is no, develop other options to breathe new life into the program.

## Lasting Value

Sometimes recognition and reward programs take on dimensions that show you just how valued they can be to employees. We once worked with a theme park that was researching various ways to put feedback and recognition into the workaday life of employees—and improve customer satisfaction in the process. On the reward and recognize side, we started giving supervisors little cards called "Warm Fuzzies" to give to employees—you guessed it—caught "doing something good." Token givers were encouraged to write notes on the backs of the cards explaining what the receiver had done to merit a Warm Fuzzie. Four years later, we had supervisors giving out Warm Fuzzies, guests giving out Warm Fuzzies, and front-line employees giving Warm Fuzzies to each other and to supervisors and staff support people.

We encountered only one problem with the system. Hoarding. Not by the givers. By the recipients. Those Warm Fuzzie cards had point values—accumulated points could be redeemed for gifts and merchandise. However, employees were not turning in the "Fuzzies" for the prizes. An employee focus group told us why. The psychological value of receiving the little cards outweighed the value of the prizes to many of the employees. As one employee put it, "When I'm having a bad day, I take out my stack of Warm Fuzzies and reread the notes on the backs, the nice things people said about me, and I feel better. That's more important than any prize I could buy for turning the cards in."

The solution was easy—give the employees credit for the points and let them keep the cards. (Made a mess of our research, but it worked.) The lesson was a big one: It's terribly easy to lose sight of how powerful a sincere "You did a good job—thanks" can be.

> The deepest principle of human nature is a craving to be appreciated.
>
> — William James
> Philosopher

# 26

# Feedback: Breakfast, Lunch, and Dinner of Champions

Hey! How'm I doin'?

—Ed Koch
Former Mayor of New York City

We all need former Mayor Koch's question answered from time to time, especially about our workaday activities. We all like to know what bosses and peers think of our performance so we have some inkling if we're on the right—or wrong—track. As a manager, your people look to you for the information they need to (1) recognize and keep doing what they do well, (2) understand and improve what they do less well, and (3) stop doing the things that contribute little to unit or organizational goals.

Information that genuinely answers those "how am I doing?" questions—that your people can use to *confirm* (call attention to good work) or *correct* (call attention to work that needs improvement) their performance—is called feedback. It comes in many forms and from a variety of sources:

- Some feedback is easy to get and hardly requires any effort to understand—charts and graphs of group and individual performance are fixtures in many workplaces.

- Some feedback is tucked away in the heads of customers—or your head as a manager. No matter how inaccessible it may seem, if your people need it to keep their performance on track, you need to get it to them, preferably while it's fresh and before it has been homogenized.

## Display Feedback

Somebody once said that if it wasn't for all the statistics, baseball would have died years ago. True or not of baseball, it says something important about human nature. We love performance data—the more tangible, visible, countable the better. How high did he jump? How far did it travel? How fast did she run? Questions like these hold endless fascination for us all.

In business, we track calls handled per hour or day, problems resolved on first contact, shipments per day, on time deliveries against standard, customers per register. Such feedback can be addictive. We love to know how we did all that today compared to yesterday, this month compared to last, in our department compared to a group in another building, or the people on another shift, or from another organization.

By using charts and graphs—the kind a normal human can decipher at a glance, not the multidimensional variety that requires a PhD in statistics to make sense of—data displays give employees valuable feedback on their performance and motivate them by the mechanisms of "confirm" and "correct."

Dr. Thomas J. Connellan is one of North America's leading authorities on the use of feedback, recognition, and reward systems in maintaining high levels of quality service. In his book, *Bringing Out the Best in Others!*,[1] Connellan identifies the six principles that the best display feedback systems follow:

1. *Feedback works best when given in relation to a specific service quality goal.* Goal-directed behavior is very powerful

---

[1]Thomas Connellan, *Bringing Out the Best in Others! 3 Keys for Business Leaders, Educators, Coaches and Parents* (Austin, TX: Bard Press, 2003).

behavior. Tell a new waiter or waitress that they waited on twenty customers tonight and the first question you'll hear is invariably, "Is that good?" Good feedback tells employees not only how they are doing, but how they are doing relative to the goals and performance standards they are expected to meet.

2. *Wherever possible, the feedback system should be managed by the people whose work created the service in the first place: front-line employees.* How many times do we put a staff rather than line person in charge of gathering, sorting, synthesizing, and circulating information on everything from delivery time, widget quality, and scrap, to customer satisfaction and employee retention? The net result is that by the time such staff-managed information gets back to where it can actually affect the service delivery system and process, it's almost always useless as confirmation or correction.

Given the right tools and a little training, front-line employees should be quite capable of gathering information on their own performance, putting it in a PowerPoint chart or graph, matching it against predetermined norms, and deciding whether or not improvement is called for. And when they do it themselves, they're more likely to believe the data, will act on it faster, and become more responsive to customers' unique needs because now they know "how they add up."

3. *Feedback should be immediate, collected, and reported as soon after the completion of the service rendered as possible.* The sooner feedback is received by the people it concerns most—the people it's about—the easier it is for them to relate their specific job behaviors to the customer's service quality or satisfaction assessment. If you were a driving instructor, you wouldn't wait until tomorrow to tell Peggy she just turned the wrong way on a one-way street. You'd want her to know how she is doing in time to keep you both from becoming someone else's statistics.

4. *Feedback should go to the person or team performing the job, not to the vice president in charge of boxes on surveys.* Obvious? Maybe. But check your current feedback practices. How long will it take for information gathered today to reach

the people at the front line? Rule of thumb: the older the data, the less useful for changing the way things get done in your service delivery system.

Let's suppose you just now decided to order four giant pepperoni pizzas as a lunch treat for the folks in your call center. How well received will your little gesture be if first the pizzas had to be signed for by a security guard two buildings away, then picked up by a mail clerk on regular office rounds, and then brought to your office for your signature before you could take them out to where you wanted them to go in the first place? How good will those pizzas taste by that time? And will you really want to be their bearer?

If Domino's and Pizza Hut can deliver direct, your feedback system can, too. Immediate, direct feedback helps your people meet their goals and targets, in the process minimizing the amount of "looking over their shoulder" corrective supervising you have to do. Remember: Autonomy and self-reliance are key components of an environment that nurtures empowered front-line workers.

5. *After it has served its immediate purpose, relevant feedback should go to all levels of the organization.* Everyone has a "need to know" when it comes to information about how the organization is performing. However, just because it's "feedback" doesn't mean it's feedback in the proper form or context. Senior management likely has no need for the level of detail that front-line employees and managers need to have to fine-tune the delivery system.

Asking "who is this information relevant to?" instead of "who would probably want to have a look at this?" is a good tool for eliminating needless paper shuffling. And the lower the proportion of useless information people see, the more attention they'll pay to information of value.

6. *Feedback should be graphically displayed.* The adage that "one picture is worth a thousand words" is certainly relevant when it comes to feedback. With the design capabilities and user-friendliness of today's software, it's easier to create compelling charts and graphs that give employees the big pic-

ture and snapshot-sharp specifics at the same time. It also provides a readily understandable comparative benchmark for
the next batch of information.

Do your people really want to know? Believe it! We
learned that lesson at the same theme park we mentioned earlier. According to the folks in the marketing department—who
had been keeping all of the info to themselves—there were
wild day-to-day variations in guest satisfaction. After much
deliberation, it was decided that "something needed to be
done."

But what? After discussing good and bad feedback methods with us, John, the human resources manager, had a 50-
foot-long by ten-foot-high wall next to the time clock turned
into a giant graph for displaying guest satisfaction scores as
measured by a 36-item survey. Instead of batch-processing
data, new survey results were added every day.

The meaning of the moving line was not lost on employees. In fact, in short order they began to ask for more detailed
survey results so they could see exactly *where* improvement
was needed. After a few weeks, the "guest satisfaction index"
began rising. And though it took occasional dips, the wild
swings in customer satisfaction were never seen again.

## Troubleshooting Your Display Feedback System

When a feedback system doesn't work, it's often because the
information gathered is being used incorrectly. It has stopped
being feedback and has become a chore, a threat, or something
to be avoided. Dr. Karen Brethower, an industrial psychologist, uses the following six questions for troubleshooting a sick
feedback system.

1. *Is the feedback being used to embarrass, punish, or
scold employees?* In one company, a "Rude Hog" award for the
service rep with the lowest customer satisfaction ratings became a badge of honor. "Way to go Harry! Don't let the SOBs
push you around" was the spirit it inspired.

2. *Is the feedback about something that has no payoff for the people receiving the information?* If there is no personal or departmental relevance to the information being collected, stop collecting it. Or at least file it under "nonessential."

3. *Is the information being provided too late for employees to act on it?* Too many things change too quickly for weeks-old or months-old information to have an effect on meaningful responses. You want to avoid giving people results from a customer satisfaction survey done six months ago.

4. *Is the feedback about something the people receiving it cannot change or effect?* You can tell a five-foot-tall person he's short, but nothing positive will come of it. Similarly, customers might report being upset about what it cost them in gas to drive to your store, but there's little your staff can do about it.

5. *Is the feedback about the wrong things?* Salespeople can't help it if customers think the store is inconveniently located or isn't decorated in a warm and friendly way. Get that feedback to someone who can act on it.

6. *Is the information difficult to collect and record?* Collecting and recording data can be a positive experience for your front-line people—unless the procedures are hellaciously difficult. We know of one company where employees rebelled against a quality improvement plan because they found the procedures so time-consuming that they were working overtime just to do their "real" jobs.

Good feedback is like a compass needle. It won't get you where you're going, but it will keep you pointed in the right direction.

Good management consists of showing average people how to do the work of superior people

—John D. Rockefeller
Industrialist and Philanthropist

# 27

# The Art of Interpersonal Feedback

People remember best those things they discover,
learn and experience themselves. The only way you
help someone accept an idea as his own is to ask a
question and let him give the answer back to you.
—Dorothy Leeds
Author and Motivational Speaker

"How am I doing?" questions often have answers that can't be meaningfully transferred to PowerPoint presentations or graphs on the wall. Interpersonal feedback is the face-to-face, manager-to-employee variation that is indispensable to an employee's morale, improvement, and growth. Mastering this vital part of your job takes courage, a good grasp of the human psyche and an overriding belief that coaching is an integral rather than peripheral function of your role as a manager.

As with "display" feedback, interpersonal feedback comes in a variety of forms:

- Some will be based on your *opinions* or point of view regarding their performance.
- Some will be based on *standards*—more formal measures and efforts that define quality performance.

Standards, in turn, come in different styles. They can be:

* Written policies or rules—"Speed limit: 65 mph."
* Unwritten but generally accepted norms—"No swimsuits worn to the office."
* Specifically negotiated between you and your employees—"For the next ninety days, we need complete data in this format on the fifteenth of each month."

Which is better: feedback based on opinions, or feedback based on standards? Either. Both. However, as you might imagine, feedback based on your opinion or point of view is much more likely to be challenged by your employees, especially if they do not agree with the feedback.

* When the patrol officer tells you that you were clocked on the radar doing 82.5 mph and you crossed a double yellow line when you passed that car, there are objective standards behind the feedback.
* But if you are stopped for "reckless driving," your judgment may be quite different than the officer's.

Whenever possible, work to coach from performance standards. They are agreed on up front and are well known to your employees. Your people will be more receptive to coaching based on concrete standards rather than on opinion or personal preference.

## Ensuring That Feedback Is Heard

The goal of providing feedback is to have it "take"—that is, make sure it is heard, valued, and hopefully used by the employee to continue or improve performance.

As a supervisor, you want *all* of your comments to matter. You know how to generate the information. But how do you improve your chances of having your people accept and act on it?

If you give feedback in a stern, parental way, you may encounter resistance because of the way your manner and tone remind your people, who now think of themselves as adults, of a very strict parent. By the same token, if you give feedback in an off-hand, flippant, "no big deal" way, your people will be inclined to view it as just that: "no big deal." The way you look and sound to your people affects how they hear, accept, and act on your message.

Two approaches can help:

1. *Work from personal expertise.* If your people respect your skill and knowledge in the area on which you are giving feedback, they're more likely to give it serious consideration, even if they disagree or feel defensive. Joe Wannabee's over-the-fence feedback on how to improve your driveway jump-shot—which you think is a game-winner—you'll probably laugh off and ignore. But if your neighbor happens to be Lebron James, you'll probably give the feedback some serious thought.

2. *Work from performance standards.* You can't compel your employees to respect your expertise. In those cases, you can increase their receptivity to corrective feedback by basing it on standards whenever possible. This takes planning. You can't announce a new standard or expectation and then immediately critique performance against it. Employees need a clear understanding of your expectations and standards. They also need time to work up to those levels. Make sure standards are set early and clearly understood if you're going to rely on them for corrective action.

Feedback must be specific and actionable to be of any use to your people. General comments like "your attitude needs improving" or "you need to listen better to your callers" will only frustrate your employees because they won't know what to do with it. Instead you might say, "I've noticed that you haven't been using the recovery process we've been stressing in our team meetings when you deal with upset customers. Apologizing is an important part of making sure customers who have problems go away happy, regardless of who is to blame. Can you help me understand why you haven't been using that part of the process?"

Giving actionable feedback often starts with asking good questions—the best advice givers are usually the best listeners. And good listeners are invariably good question askers.

"John, I had a call from Mr. Sanchez. He's been a valued customer over the years, and I'd like us to help him if we can. He was a little upset with his last conversation with you. So I need to understand what this is all about. Could you summarize the situation for me?"

Mr. Sanchez, it turns out, wanted some additional time to make a payment, and didn't care much for John's response—which essentially stated company policy.

Manager/coach: "What alternatives do you think the customer would have been able to accept in this situation?"

Once you've explored options with John, you can help him select the next step. "It sounds like there are a couple of alternatives you can offer him. Which one do you want to propose first?"

Open-ended questions are generally more useful for coaching scenarios than the close-ended variety. Some examples:

> "What was the customer upset about?
> "What have you tried so far?"
> "What can I do to help?"
> "What would you like to accomplish when you call her back?"
> "How do you think you might you plan your work more effectively?"

## Giving Clear Feedback

Here are six steps to help you plan clear feedback:

1. *Specify what the task is and why it is important to the unit or team.* Discuss the benefit to the team or unit if the task is accomplished well and the consequences to the unit or team if it is not.

2. *Determine what other work is currently being done and mutually agree on how improvement efforts in this area rank in priority to other tasks or responsibilities.* Customer contact employees usually have plenty on their plates, and providing guidance on which tasks or

goals you see as the most critical can help bring a sense of order to their multitasking.

3. *Agree on a standard.* Make sure it covers all elements of the task, such as completion time, quality expected, quantity expected, and decide which element is most important.
4. *Discuss the resources (time and materials) needed for the task and agree on what actions should be taken to meet these requirements.*
5. *Discuss: (1) what you believe a person would need to know and be able to do in order to do the task well, (2) your view of the individual employee's abilities, and (3) the employee's self-assessment of task and abilities.* This is important. You may learn that an employee doesn't possess the necessary skill or knowledge to accomplish a task or meet a service standard, and some additional training or coaching will be needed.
6. *In concert with the employee, jointly establish the methods to be used to monitor progress, solve problems related to the task, and evaluate the final result.*

Feedback is the breakfast, lunch, and dinner of champions because it feeds growth and success. Winners like to hear plenty of "you're the greatest" confirming feedback. Winners also know that getting better comes with feedback that helps them see their performance in the context of long-term goals.

Good feedback takes effective planning. It becomes more effective and powerful the more it is sincerely given and is based on clear expectations and standards. And like breakfast, lunch, and dinner, you need to provide it on a regular basis.

The wise leader does not try to protect people from themselves. The light of awareness shines equally on what is pleasant and on what is not pleasant.

—John Heider
*The Tao of Leadership*

# 28

# Celebrate Success

I have yet to find the man, however exalted his station,
who did not do better work and put forth greater effort
under a spirit of approval than under a spirit of criticism.
—Charles Schwab
Founder, Charles Schwab Corporation

Celebration serves a variety of functions in an organization.
On the simplest level, it is a form of recognition and reward.
That in and of itself is an important function, a worthy pur-
pose.

However, celebration is also a way of nourishing group
spirit. It represents a moment in time when a glimpse of a
transformed organization—a product of the efforts of people
from many levels—can be seen, felt, and enjoyed. In highly
human terms, celebration reaffirms to people that they are an
important part of something that really matters.

For most people, the feeling of being part of something
important and meaningful is a powerful motivator. Being part
of a "winning team," being seen as the best in the industry,
achieving something others admire and respect become a
power that can make salary increases, bonuses, generous 401K
plans, and even the most carefully designed perk program
seem lackluster by comparison.

Celebration reminds everyone that purposes and goals not
only exist, but are exciting, important, and attainable.
Reconfirming to people at all levels in your organization that
they are part of something important, that the service they pro-

vide is vital to both the organization and the people they serve may be the most important motivational principle of all.

Celebration should be an integral part of the way you recognize and reward good performance. To make it effective, pay attention to *when* you celebrate, *why* you celebrate, with *whom* you celebrate, and *how* you celebrate.

## When

Timing is a key variable in a multitude of service activities, and celebration is no exception. As with other forms of reinforcement, "the quicker the better" is one good rule of thumb. It's hard for people to get realistically happy in December over something they did last June. Following are some good times to celebrate.

1. *When you need to mark the end of a project or major effort.* Achievers (those who take pride in a job well done) often have a need for closure, the knowledge that their efforts have led to a visible conclusion. When the work just goes on and on, lack of closure can burn them out. Achievers need to know they've achieved, in other words. In the absence of natural closure, invent it: "Fifty days without . . . ," "three quarters in a row during which we . . . ," the tenth (one-hundredth?) positive customer letter.

2. *When you are making a transition from one stage to another.* Celebration can not only mark the end of one phase, it can acknowledge the beginning of a new one, reinforcing new goals and standards with the recognition that the last ones proved eminently doable.

3. *When your unit has met an important goal.* Whether short- or long-term, goals achieved in business should be like goals scored in a soccer or hockey game: an occasion for a few immediate "high fives" before the game resumes in earnest. If you meet monthly targets for resolving customer problems on first contact or quarterly goals for on-time deliveries, celebrate with

something beyond a "nice job" for the troops. Spontaneity is as important in celebrating as planning. Sometimes you'll have the champagne on ice. Other times, you'll just want to savor the unexpected moment in whatever way seems best at the time.

## Why

Picking your spots is important. So, too, is having a reason for the celebration. Without a strategic component, celebrations can become trivialized or wind up reinforcing the wrong things. Following are some good reasons to celebrate.

1. *To motivate.* Celebrating obviously lends passion to the rational, emotion to the logical, and joy to the somber. It rekindles the spirit and leaves a warm glow that can endure long after the moment has passed. It pumps air back into the organizational balloon.
2. *To model.* Celebrations create a forum or setting that can be used to tell the stories of new service heroes. By making good examples of your people, others on the service team gain a deeper understanding of the attitudes and actions you want them to emulate.
3. *To communicate priorities.* Just as what gets rewarded gets repeated, what you decide to celebrate showcases your priorities. If the reasons you select involve cost-cutting, budget-reducing, and general frugality, your people will know to pinch pennies. If service excellence is the consistent theme, in contrast, you'll make it very clear that working for customers is at the top of your list.
4. *To encourage.* Sales organizations know the value of motivational sales rallies that renew the spirit of people whose job entails hearing no in every variation known to man (and woman). Service people endure similar stresses, and often without the counterbalance of sales successes. Celebrations help recharge service batteries drawn down by the emotional labor of dealing with difficult customers.

## Who

Celebrations are for people, by people. The human element has a lot of dimensions, including those that follow.

1. *Your Role as Manager.* This is one occasion where it's better to lead than delegate. Sure, it's important to get others involved. However, you miss an important and necessary opportunity and can actually send the wrong message by taking an "I'll just stay here in the background" position. You do not have to be a charismatic, back-slapping cheerleader type to lead the effort. Be yourself, but be up front—that's how your people know the celebration is truly meaningful to you.

2. *Their Role as Participants.* Basically, the more the better. There are times for small, intimate gatherings of a chosen few. However, times of celebration aren't among them. Err on the side of too many people rather than too few. Let everyone bask in the warmth of success.

3. *The Prominence of Contributors.* Involve everyone who contributed in the cause for celebration. The key word is "contributed." You don't want to muddy the celebratory waters by giving credit to people where none is due, but you also don't want to recognize only a few of the many who played a part. It's even worth the risk of an Oscar night marathon. For recipients, the chance to be acknowledged, and to use their "moment in the sun" to acknowledge those who contributed to their achievements, outweighs where the big and little hands are on the clock.

4. *The Appearance of Special Guests.* You compliment your people and your guests when you reinforce the importance of the celebration by inviting others. Consider including a few key customers or vendors, or people from another department on which your people rely. A caveat: Defer to the feelings of the celebrants in bringing in outsiders—the unexpected appearance of someone they have good reason to label a "customer from hell" can throw cold water in their faces.

## How

There's no one right way to celebrate. In fact, try to explore different forms of celebration to keep things from becoming routine and predictable. (You can, to be sure, have worse problems than getting yourself into a "celebrations rut" because of your continuing stream of successes.) A few guidelines follow.

1. *Keep it upbeat.* Celebrations should be fun, they should be positive in nature, and they should avoid things your celebrants find boring (such as the shopworn "chicken-a-la-Goodyear" meal and attendant boring speeches and bad jokes). Make the event festive and fun. Get lots of ideas by getting lots of people involved in the planning and execution.
2. *Use lasting symbols.* Find tangible ways to preserve the moment: hats and t-shirts, banners, a video that tells the story (or, better yet, lets those who did the deed tell the story), a write-up in internal publications, special plaques, or keepsakes.
3. *Make it classy.* Aim for celebrations that are public, not private; open, not closed; spontaneous, not scheduled to the minute; and inclusive, not elitist. They should reflect organizational values start to finish.
4. *Recognize and reward.* Pull the celebration together around the people and the achievements you're recognizing. Otherwise, it's just another party.

## Some Noteworthy Celebrations

• When Bill Daiger of Maryland National Bank wanted his front-line people to know that he and the bank appreciated their efforts to make MNB number one in customer service, he hired a hall, sent out formal invitations, and threw a magnificent party for all employees. The affair was such a hit that the bank now regularly takes time to throw a party and celebrate its "stars."

• At Netflix, the online DVD subscription service based in Los Gatos, California, managers celebrate hitting targets for new subscribers to the company's "Friends" network, which gives customers a glimpse at how their friends have reviewed movies they've seen, with Friday afternoon potluck lunches. Managers publicly thank all those who had a hand in achieving the goal, and employees have a chance to socialize and sample creative dishes their colleagues have cooked up.

• Hartsford Jackson Atlanta International Airport throws an annual celebration recognizing the outstanding efforts by airport personnel—encompassing all airlines, and other airport services. Winners' stories are shared and tales range from assisting a pregnant woman give birth in an airport restroom, to ensuring children get on the right flight, to going the extra mile ensuring a passenger gets the individualized care they require. Prizes range from plaques, dinner gift certificates, hi definition televisions, trips, and even a new car. It is a day filled with fun, frivolity and inspiration.

• At LensCrafters, they celebrate the end of store-level sales contest in a unique fashion. The awards meeting starts in a familiar way. Performance awards are passed out, customer compliment letters read aloud, and individual employees saluted by the regional manager. As the meeting winds to a close, however, a unique (and greatly anticipated) twist occurs. The individual with the best contest record closes the meeting by serving up a cream pie straight into the mug of a designated recipient—point blank, no ducking, no begging off—whopp!

Don't ask. Some organizational traditions and symbols aren't meant to be understood by outsiders.

> We have lots of celebrations. We create a lot of situations in which employees are brought before their peers and recognized.
>
> —Ed Crutchfield
> Former CEO, First Union Corporation

# Imperative 8

## Your Most Important Management Mission: Set the Tone and Lead the Way

It's sometimes hard to believe that you have any "power" over anyone in your organization. Or that very much of what you say, let alone what you do, has much influence over other people's behavior. However, looks can be deceiving.

The people who think of you as "the boss" are more than a little swayed by your actions. Like it or not, you are the personal role model for many of the people who work for you. How they see you deal with and talk about, peers, colleagues, employees, and customers tells them what the real rules of conduct are for your part of the organization.

You can't con or manipulate people into doing quality work or caring about their customers. You *can* lead them there. Your personal example of doing things right, of taking the time to listen to customers and employees with patience, and focusing your energy on things that say "quality service" to your customers—internal and external—are critical parts of your leadership role. You, by your day-to-day example and leadership, set the tone and lead the way.

> If you are serious about product quality and customer service, and you're not spending 35 percent of your time on it (by gross calendar analysis), then you are not serious about it.
>
> —Tom Peters
> Management Guru

# 29

# Manager-Employee Trust: Ground Zero for Service Quality

The people in the 5- by 5-foot cubicles won't put themselves on the line with customers if they don't trust the
organization they work for.

—Napolean Barrigan
Founder and CEO of 1-800-Mattress

It's an unfortunate truism that most employees don't trust their leaders. The lingering fallout from Enron, WorldCom, and other corporate debacles still has front liners casting side-long glances and thinking dark thoughts about those in the management ranks. However, it's not only top executives who are the targets of suspicion. Studies show middle managers and supervisors increasingly find their credibility and trust-worthiness under question as well. "Can I trust the people I work for to look after me, keep their word, and honor their promises, or is it everyone for themselves?" "Will my supervi-sor have my back if a customer makes an unfounded or frivolous charge about service I provided?" "Are they telling us everything they know about this proposed merger?" Rank-and-file workers are beginning to believe that trust in the busi-ness world is a sham.

Such aspersions aren't always well-grounded, of course; everyone likes to cop out with "this place would be better if managers would just..." from time to time, lumping all leaders in the same sinister category. Yet perception is a powerful thing, and a lack of trust between managers and employees can cripple morale and poison efforts to deliver distinctive service quality. When front liners don't feel the boss "has their back," it's hard for them to summon the energy, good cheer, and emotional resilience to give customers their best each day. When management doesn't trust employees, it not only affects front-line performance it shows through to customers. Customers like dealing with empowered employees; in fact, they believe the attitude of the entire organization is reflected in the authority given the front line. If they deal with employees who seem to be distrusted by the organization, they assume they will be treated the same.

It's easy to see, then, why building a culture of trust is one of the most important things you can do as a manager.

## The High Cost of Mistrust

The cost of low trust within an organization or business unit is obvious and subtle. A number of studies performed over the past 15 years have found that when employees distrust the organization or manager they work for they contribute less effort to the job, take fewer risks, are more cynical about the company's plans and promises, and are more likely to leave when other opportunities arise. There also is evidence of a direct relationship between employee trust and the bottom line. A 2002 study by global consulting firm Watson Wyatt Worldwide found that "companies with the highest employee trust scores post 42 percent higher shareholder returns" than others in the research.

A review of twenty-five individual studies and several literature reviews makes three things abundantly clear: (1) Trust is critically important to the workplace and the marketplace; (2) Trust is as much perceptual as it is a performance issue; and (3) Trust in an individual—whether your front-line staff trusts you, for example—is different from trust in the organization as a whole.

## Hope for Change

Amid the turmoil and growing suspicion there continue to be managers and supervisors that employees would trust with their newborn children. These leaders engender such a strong sense of loyalty and commitment that their "followers" would likely continue working for them even in the face of below-market pay, lack of promotional opportunities or the absence of other traditional job perks. In a word, they are seen as trustworthy—even by those who routinely tell pollsters of corporate leaders, "You can't trust the scoundrels."

These bosses succeed by demonstrating character in ways their people accept as genuine and rely on as real. They regularly display a handful of traits that create dedicated followers: authenticity, candor, fairness, accessibility, and supportiveness. All of which combine to create a powerful cocktail of credibility.

Jim Kouzes, coauthor of *The Leadership Challenge and Credibility: How Leaders Gain and Lose It*, is a preeminent leadership researcher who has studied corporate managers for more than 20 years. If there's a recurring theme from the research he and colleague Barry Posner have done, it's this: Credibility is the foundation of leadership, and without it efforts to lead others are usually doomed to failure. "People won't believe the message if they don't believe in the messenger," Kouzes says. "Credibility essentially is doing what you say you are going to do. You can't stand up in front of people and announce policies you are not willing to personally implement, or make promises you know in your heart you can't keep."

Here are the traits consistently exhibited by trust-inspiring managers:

- *They are authentic.* Why is authenticity essential to building trust? "An authentic leader is trusted by employees

*(Text continues on page 215)*

### How Renewed Trust Reversed One Ship's Fortunes

When D. Mike Abrashoff took over command of the USS Benfold, a U.S. Navy guided missile destroyer, in 1997 morale and trust levels on the ship couldn't have been any lower. The Benfold was a brand new, billion dollar technological wonder, but crew members couldn't transfer off of it fast enough. Yet by the end of Abrashoff's tenure as skipper, sailors from other ships were clamoring to join his crew.

The twenty-one-month turnaround documented in his book, *It's Your Ship: Management Techniques From the Best Damn Ship in the Navy* (Warner Business Books, 2002) offers insights applicable to any organization where lack of trust is undermining harmony and threatening productivity or service quality levels. Here are some key learnings from Abrashoff's successful journey to a high-trust environment:

- *When in trouble, hear your crew out.* Abrashoff emphasizes the importance of listening without prejudice to all hands. He asked every one of his 310 crewmen the same nine personal and work-related questions, from "Is there anything the Navy can do to help your family?" to "What would you change on the Benfold if you could?" He then acted immediately on the things he could control—like arranging counseling for crew members' families facing financial strife.
- *Don't accept standard operating procedure at face value.* Abrashoff asked "why" about virtually everything—and changed what didn't make sense or what crew members believed they could do a better way. The belief that everyone can make a difference rippled through the ranks. Many "make work" duties were eliminated or simplified, for example. The trust lesson? The simple act of listening to employees and acting on their best ideas generates trust and confidence in leadership.
- *Cultivate quality of work life.* In Abrashoff's mind nothing was out of bounds for boosting morale and building trust. He started a karaoke happy hour and showed music videos projected on the side of the ship

to provide regular distractions from often tedious ship duties. He also arranged for GED tutors to be flown to the ship and created a distance learning center on-board for college level courses for crew members seeking to further their educations. If it made life a lit-tle more interesting or entertaining, he tried it.

- *Focus on your people, not your next promotion.* Abrashoff worked from the premise that if he took care of his ship and its crew, his career would take care of itself. He believes that attitude freed him to make some of the changes he did. "When your orga-nizing principle is performance, not obedience, things change," he says.

By the time Abrashoff was reassigned (promoted) the Benfold had won the Spokane Trophy for having the best combat readiness in the fleet. His re-up rate (crew members retained) increased from 30 percent to 100 percent. And there was a long waiting list of sailors petitioning for assign-ment to the Benfold.

because they know that leader understands what his or her strengths and weaknesses are, and won't put the unit or com-pany at risk by stepping into something they aren't prepared to deal with," says Kevin Cashman, founder and CEO of Leadersource, a leadership development firm in Minneapolis. "We trust them because we know they won't put up a façade."

Authentic leaders also demonstrate humility. Humility doesn't mean publicly falling on your sword, nor does it imply loudly advertising your own warts or clay feet. It also doesn't mean going overboard with self-effacing comments—too much humbleness undermines the confidence employees have in you. It *does* mean working hard to be more open and vulnera-ble with your employees and staying alert for opportunities to show empathy. It also entails working to strip any nuance of rank or status from the relationship. Great manager-employee relationships tend to be egalitarian, not laced with sovereignty.

• *They are forthright, fair, and keep their promises.*
Candor, telling it like it is with your people, is an essential
building *block* of trust. "Leaders gain a lot of credibility with
the troops by honest acknowledgement of what's really happening in the organization," says Nick Morgan, head of the
communications skills coaching company Public Words in
Boston. Whether it's the state of the company's finances, the
latest customer satisfaction, or retention data or during a performance appraisal, managers build trust by telling it straight
rather than relying on half-truths or sugarcoating the facts.
The reality is most of your employees have finely calibrated
"crap detectors" and can usually sniff out such shiftiness even
when not directly downwind.

Candor also means telling people you don't know what
will happen—be it a downsizing, merger, or other news that
has the rumor mill churning, rather than making false assur-
ances or promises.

Trust also is built by fairness—by not letting star performers play by their own rules and by dealing head-on with any
team members who aren't pulling their weight. When people
believe the playing field is slanted in someone's favor, trust
flies out the window.

Finally, trust is established by diligently honoring your
promises, keeping commitments, and accepting responsibility
for company policy. Nothing corrodes trust as quickly as making Lucy-to-Charlie Brown-style promises to your people, holding out the football then jerking it away right before it's kicked.
Whether it's the promise of a pay raise, more flexible work hours,
new computer technology—or "firing" a particularly nasty customer—don't make it unless you know you can deliver.

• *They are accessible and establish clear expectations.*
Managers who engender trust spend plenty of time being visible and interacting with their staff, working hard to live up to
the "people before paperwork" pledge. They understand that
nothing beats face-to-face, personal contact for creating trust
between people. They also honor the importance of crystal-
clear communication—they strive to give clear assignments,
offer specific, actionable performance feedback, and set ambitious but realistic goals. They know the danger of working by

the "I'll know it when I see it" method of defining good performance. When employees know upfront what's expected of them, and understand the specific skills, attitudes, and results that separate mediocre from exemplary performance, there are few excuses for not getting the job done.

- *They support their people in trying times.* Trustworthy managers never sacrifice their people to protect their own hides or to look good in front of customers. When your employees feel you'll put yourself at risk for them, their trust level grows.

If an upset customer blows his top about service he received from someone on staff, these managers take a deep breath and investigate before rushing to judgment—even if the employee has faced similar accusations before. First they make sure the customer gets what he or she needs to remedy the situation, and then they meet privately with the staff member to get his side of the story. Any corrective coaching is done in private. Similarly, when there's a conflict brewing on the customer contact staff—charges of someone not pulling their weight, for example—the trust-engendering manager goes first to the accused to hear his explanation rather than calling a team pow-wow and risking a conflagration. Experience tells the manager he might just find that a personal or health-related issue is causing a temporary drop-off in productivity or service quality. If it's a matter of motivation, attitude or training, he'll address the problem differently.

Putting the "us" in trust involves remembering that trust is an interpersonal dimension. Trust is something which happens *within* people only when it is created *between* people. However, it doesn't happen by accident or good intentions— trust is crafted "by hand" every day in the many decisions you make and actions you take in leading your front-line staff.

The glue that holds all relationships together, including the relationship between the leader and the led, is trust, and trust is based on integrity.

—Brian Tracy
Professional Speaker and Sales Trainer

# 30

# Observation Is More Powerful Than Conversation

People learn more from observation than they do from conversation.

—Will Rogers
American Humorist

Though cowboy humorist Will Rogers had politicians on the mind at the time—and how their actions tell more about their real thoughts and values than any campaign speech or promise ever could—his quip has turned out to be true of most human beings. Actions *do* speak much louder than words.

There is even a body of scientific knowledge, which psychologists call Behavior Modeling, that speaks about the way the behavior of parents, teachers, sports figures, television and movie actors, and rock stars influences the behavior of children—and the way the behavior of supervisors and managers influences the people who report to them, take instructions from them, and look to them for guidance, support, and recognition.

The message for managers is clear:

What your people see you doing, day in and day out, sends a more powerful and convincing message about what is important to you and the organization than any e-mail you could ever write, any speech you could ever make, or any clever motivational message you could ever post on the bulletin board. The way you treat customers, vendors, your peers, and your employees sets the "real rules" of the organization.

In short, whether you know it or not and whether you like it or not: *You* are the message.

If your employees hear you talking about "those #&*@ customers . . . If they'd just take their darned questions somewhere else, maybe we'd get some work done around here!" they walk away with two lessons learned. First, that customers are pests. Second, that it's okay to treat them like the plague rather than the purpose of the business.

If your employees see you chewing out another employee in public, or witness you questioning a peer's sanity for trying to accomplish something unusual for a customer, there are a number of possible lessons learned vicariously. Things like: "Don't put yourself out for a customer—it just leads to trouble with the boss," and "Must be okay to hassle people when they don't do exactly what you want—the boss does it all the time."

## Hints for Making Yourself an Effective Model

*Question:* Want to know how to make your people better listeners?
*Answer:* Become a better listener yourself. Make sure they see you practicing active listening skills—with customers, with your peers, and with your people.
*Question:* Want your people to work better together? To be better team players?
More cooperative? More prone to give and take and less prone to demands and "positions"?
*Answer:* Encourage and demonstrate teamwork. Become a better team player with your own peers. Reward and draw attention to good examples of teamwork when they occur. Treat your employees as members of your team and envelop them in the practice of what you are preaching, just the way any good coach would.

*Question:* Want your people to deliver better service to customers?

*Answer:* You already know the answer, but for the book: be seen serving customers with the enthusiasm, skill, and attentiveness you expect your people to exhibit.

And be seen treating your internal customers, your peers, the people who support your efforts, and the people who depend on you for support—your employees—with respect, care, and attention.

First Union Bank, part of First Union Corporation (which merged with Wachovia Corp. in 2001 and then kept its name) was the most profitable bank in the United States in the late 1980s. And one of the most consciously customer service oriented. However, that wasn't always the case. Not too many years earlier, First Union had a pretty mediocre service reputation among its customers.

We asked Edward E. Crutchfield, Jr., CEO and chairman of First Union at the time, how the bank went from just so-so to the status of an acknowledged service superior organization. He scarcely missed a beat at the question. His management "secret" is, he says, no secret at all. Will Rogers said it shorter, but he certainly didn't say it any better:

*"Service sinks in when managers talk and act service, service, service, day in and day out in obvious and in subtle ways."*

You must be the change you wish to see in the world."

—Mahatma Gandi
Political and Spiritual Leader
of the Indian Independence
Movement

# 31

# Great Service Leadership in Action

*Lead, follow, or get out of the way.*
—Sign on a Marine Corps Training Center Door

Sure, we're supposed to be role models. We know all about making service excellence a priority and how we need to communicate the service vision," they chided. "But, that's just consultant-talk. What does "being a service leader" look like up close on a Monday morning when all heck breaks loose in the call center or on the sales floor?

Remembering the lessons from Consulting 101, we chose a small group exercise as a way of answering the question. "Assume you implemented today a new unconditional service guarantee," we instructed the group. "The service guarantee promised that if customers were not completely happy with the service experience—how they were treated, they would get a refund equal to ten times the price paid for the product or service. What actions would you take to avoid quickly going bankrupt?"

The mood in the room shifted from skepticism to feverish brainstorming. Even the quieter members began filling up flipcharts with leader actions aimed at keeping the service spirit alive and employees focused on taking care of customers. When the exercise was completed, the twelve managers had generated over a hundred specific "Monday morning" actions. And in the process discovered their own answers to the "walking the talk" question.

We compared their list against what we have witnessed from leaders known for inspiring, instigating, and sustaining a culture famous for service. Some have names that identify their enterprise—Bruce Nordstrom, Debbi Fields, Michael Dell, and Bill Marriott. Others are known only to their associates, stockholders, and customers. Their actions have similar themes.

## They Connect

"He's everywhere," say people of Ed Fuller, president of Marriott International, the customer-centric hotel chain. The words aren't just about a man who literally travels the globe each month visiting Marriott properties. It's the way Fuller takes time out to greet a Marriott bellman he met on a previous trip, to ask the "Was it a boy or girl?" question of the front desk clerk who was pregnant on his last visit or to tell a story about the exemplary service delivered by a banquet supervisor in the presence of her general manager. Fuller's openness, enthusiasm and authentic curiosity about employees' work and personal lives helps him connect in a way that leaves a powerful impression—one of a leader who understands and values the hard work front liners put in every day serving customers.

Effective service leaders avoid getting "stuck in meetings." Try to schedule a sit down meeting with Larry Kurzweil, president of Universal Studios Hollywood, and you're likely to hear, "Sure we can meet. You don't mind if we walk the park while we talk, do you?" Kurzweil's attentive listening is punctuated with stops to ask questions of associates or give directions to guests. It's almost like Universal runs on Larry's supercharged battery and if he's not out there meeting, greeting, and energizing, the park will deflate and go flat. Being visible, making yourself available to answer staff questions, pitching in to serve customers during busy times—and opting to communicate face-to-face rather than relying on e-mail whenever possible—all help foster trust by creating the sense you're working alongside the troops, not tucked safely away in "management-only" bunker far from the action.

## They Support

Service leadership in the past meant control and consistency. The "boss" of yesteryear kept a tight rein, otherwise employees would "get lazy and fail to work." We know now that employees act like adults when they are treated like adults. Employees who manage a tight personal budget, buy and sell real estate, prepare complex tax returns—not to mention successfully juggle schedules filled with soccer games, dentist appointments, or part-time college classes—likely have the wisdom and experience to handle almost any work assignment. At home, they don't need any one ensuring they're "empowered" or have "appropriate supervision."

The service leader's role is to support and serve employees. That means running interference and getting people the resources they need so they can consistently work at a high level; it also means supporting and coaching them—not just assigning blame—when they've had difficult interactions with upset or insensitive customers.

As a service leader you're still in charge of control and consistency, of course. However, it's a goal you pursue *with* employees, not something you *impose* on them. If your people are clear on unit and organizational goals, if they know what's expected to accomplish service standards and norms—and understand the "why's" behind all those objectives—they will help you ensure control and consistency if allowed. Effective leaders always look for ways to involve, include, and invite their employees in service delivery.

## They Listen

Knowing that listening to your people is important and *being* a good listener are two very different things. Ask employees about the listening skills of their bosses and most will give them a failing grade. Why is it that with an infinite number of books and articles written on the topic employees continue to ding their leaders on their listening skills? We think the problem has less to do with *communication* management and much more to do with *noise* management.

Most leaders *can* be great listeners. Let their seven-year-old come crying about a neighborhood conflict and you will see great listening. Zero in on a corner conversation they're having in a funeral home during the wake of a friend and you will see great listening. Yet mix the normal pace and chaos of a work day with the typical "I'm the boss" persona—and the mindset that "employees don't need to be babied"—and you have a prescription for the just-get-to-the-punch-line type listening we see with too many leaders.

The sounds of great listening tell us effective listeners don't start doing anything special, but they do stop doing something normal—they don't even attempt to listen when they know they can't provide undivided attention. "Hold my calls," "let's get out of here so we can really talk," or "Tell him I'll have to call back" are words that telegraph noise management. They say to employees, "What you have to say is so important, I don't want to miss a word." If you can't give your people that kind of focus, postpone the encounter until you can. It's better to say, "Tom, I want to give you my complete attention, but I'm an hour from a crucial meeting and I would honestly only be giving you half of my attention. Can we schedule this later today when I can really focus?" Then make sure you live up to that promise.

A wise leader once said, "There are no individuals at work who are more important to your success than your employees . . . not your boss, not your customers, not your vendors." Make sure your listening practices reflect that truism.

## They Enrich

"Add value to every moment by taking it personal," was the advice we heard Greg Haller, president of the Midwest Region for Verizon Wireless, give to associates at an employee rally near Detroit. The words come from a man renowned for his passion for customer service. Great service leaders always look for small ways to add value—instead of barking an order or sending an e-mail directive, they inspire by telling a story of how someone in the organization thrilled a customer by quickly or creatively resolving a tough problem. Instead of determining how well the organization is serving customers by reading customer satisfaction reports, they get out on the front lines and find out face-to-face, talking to customer contact employees, and interacting with clients. They abhor excuses, blame, or any actions that acquiesce to the status quo rather than altering it in the name of improved service.

Your people—your followers—take their cue from you. You influence how they feel about the organization as a whole, about your unit in particular, about the type of work they do, about customers and about themselves. What you value, they will value. While that may seem a heavy burden to bear, setting the tone and modeling good service behaviors are the very essence of being a good leader.

## They Inspire

Don Freeman, chairman of the Freeman Companies, speaks from "the heart instead of a chart" when he addresses his managers about taking the courageous step of changing the Freeman culture to one focused on building customer loyalty. A leading full service contractor for expositions and conventions, Dallas-based Freeman has long delivered exemplary service to its key customers—those who manage and coordinate shows. To grow the company, Freeman knew it would have to build an equally strong reputation with customers who exhibit at shows, not just show managers. In response to customer suggestions, Freeman opened a new customer support center as one way to do that. "Unlike some call centers where the primary purpose is to take orders, our center is designed to assist exhibitors with show service questions and quickly resolve their issues," says center manager Brenda McCord.

Don Freeman, like other effective service leaders, knows how important it is for leaders to set the mood, tone, and tenor of the company, buoy people's spirits and enlist them in a cause. At the same time, he understands that few people want to work for a "cheerleader" boss—the kind of visionless manipulator who simply enjoys the sound of his own voice and the thrill of talking others into doing his bidding. People will volunteer to work for bosses, however, who are at their inspirational best during tough times, who model the behaviors they ask others to show with customers, and who take time to coach and support rather than berate or blame when things go awry on the front lines.

## They Offer a Strategy of Optimism and Tenacity

The service quality journey is not always easy. In fact, it is often tough and discouraging. The new computer hardware or software you installed frustrates rather than helps. One of your most valuable customers tells you to take a hike after a less-than-model conversation with your most experienced and trusted employee. Two of your new hires simply stop showing up for work. And you learn that your unit will face a significant budget reduction in the next biennium. This is the time when effective leaders draw optimism and tenacity from their followers—and give it back tenfold.

Effective leaders know the wisdom of the maxim, "abandon all hope for a better yesterday." They lift spirits by always focusing on a better tomorrow, understanding the folly of dwelling on past mistakes or miscalculations. When the pressure is on and the stakes are high, effective service leaders also set the standard for their organizations. As any parent knows who has hammered a finger instead of a nail with an observant child present, modeling is most memorable and powerful when under pressure.

Great leaders connect, support, enrich, inspire, and provide hope. They also patiently listen to employees, customers and vendors in a constant quest for service improvement. Bottom line, great service leaders achieve that status because of one overriding quality: They *serve*.

> I find the great thing in this world is, not where we stand, but in what direction we are moving.
>
> —Oliver Wendell Holmes
> American Jurist

# Index

227

# About the Authors

**Chip Bell** is the founder of The Chip Bell Group, headquartered near Dallas. Prior to starting the firm in 1980, he was Director of Management Development and Training for NCNB (now Bank of America). Dr. Bell is the author or coauthor of such best-selling books as *Magnetic Service, Customers as Partners, Managers as Mentors,* and *Service Magic.* His work has been featured on CNN, CNBC, Bloomberg TV, and in the *Wall Street Journal, Fortune, USA Today, Fast Company,* and *Business Week.* A renowned keynote speaker, he has served as consultant or trainer to many Fortune 100 companies.

**Ron Zemke** was one of the primary leaders of the American customer service revolution. His writings and research on the organizational impact of customer service are considered landmark. Prior to Ron's untimely death in 2004, he authored or coauthored more than 35 books including *Service America in the New Economy,* the entire *Knock Your Socks Off Service* series, *E-Service,* and *Generations at Work.* He was Senior Editor of *TRAINING* magazine, a syndicated columnist for the *American City Business Journals,* and host of five films about the service management process.

**Dave Zielinski** is a freelance writer and editor who specializes in business management, customer service, and human resource topics. He has contributed to most of the *Knock Your Socks Off Service* series, as well as to numerous other service books from Performance Research Associates.